BY Barbara Miller With Charles Paul Conn
Kathy
BY Barbara and Kathy Miller
We're Gonna Win

We're Gonna Win

Barbara Miller
Kathy Miller

FLEMING H. REVELL COMPANY
OLD TAPPAN, NEW JERSEY

Scripture quotations in this volume are from the King James Version of the Bible.

Library of Congress Cataloging in Publication Data

Miller, Barbara, date
  We're gonna win.
  1. Miller, Barbara. 2. Miller,
Kathy. 3. Methodists—United States—Biography.
4. Christian life—Methodist authors. I. Miller,
Kathy. II. Title.
BX8493.M5   1983   248.4′876   82-18565
ISBN 0-8007-1340-0

Kathy and I join in appreciation acknowledging Charlotte Hale Allen as writer of this book. Charlotte's willingness to lend her encouragement, excitement, and love to the project has been a real gift to us. Her personal commitment to Jesus Christ is the basis of her desire to have this book be all that God intends it to be.

In loving memory of our Mother/Grandmother
Doris M. Barlow
We're grateful for her cooperation and effort
in unlocking doors that will allow other
mother-daughter relationships to become
functional and meaningful.

Contents

Foreword

Our family's story has touched many hearts. The book *Kathy*, written by my wife, Barbara, with Charles Paul Conn, has been translated into half a dozen other languages since its publication in 1980. I continue to be amazed at the people it reaches.

The story of Kathy Miller's physical, mental, and emotional comeback—miraculous and moving as it is—proved to be just the tip of the iceberg. The ten-and-one-half-week coma Kathy entered on March 14, 1977, left a devastated shell of the girl we'd known before her tragic accident. Her trauma in fact overwhelmed our entire family, leaving our individual and collective futures very much in doubt.

As Barbara, Larry Don, and I worked to help Kathryn Suzanne Miller relearn everything she once had known, we saw God Himself reprogram Kathy. Not only did I regain the daughter I thought I'd lost forever, she came back as an even better person than she was before.

The miracle I watched God perform was a day-by-day, step-by-step process which seemed excruciatingly slow. Barbara, exhibiting unwavering courage, faith, and tenacity, became the primary vehicle He used to restructure Kathy's mind and personality.

Kathy recovered. That should be enough. But God was not through with us yet. As Barbara poured herself into the

11

daughter doctors said would live as a vegetable, we watched an astonishing mother-daughter relationship develop. Daily, Barbara would tell Kathy, "With God's help, you're gonna win." Soon our daughter tried to talk; first words, then sentences. I remember her struggles to enunciate in that slurred, toneless speech, "I'm gonna win."

The victory went far beyond all we could ask or even think. The radiant, loving mother-daughter team exuded a supernatural kind of caring, patience, and faith that changed not only Kathy's life, but then Barbara's, eventually Larry Don's, and finally my own.

I watched the Christ in Barbara minister to Kathy, pull out the very best in her. I saw the power of love in action. Daily I watched God at work. What I saw brought me into a new relationship to Jesus Christ. It inspired me to work—really work—for the first time in my life on relating in depth to my wife and our struggling son. God brought Barbara and me away from the brink of divorce. God saved our only son, whom we were losing to drugs and alcohol.

When Kathy was five or six weeks into her coma, I recall sitting beside the bed of this frail, emaciated little girl the doctors said would die, or forever be a "vegetable," and I'd ask, "God, what is the meaning of this? What possible good can come out of such hideous tragedy?"

My prayers for Kathy's future were so modest. I underestimated God, for His plans for Kathy's future were far beyond my expectations. Imagine if someone had come to me in those days and said, "Your daughter will come out of this coma. Within six months she will complete a ten-thousand-meter race. She'll graduate from high school on schedule, with honors.

"Kathy will be awarded an international trophy for

Valour in Sport given to one athlete per year, winning over a field of eight hundred entrants from one hundred twenty countries. She'll win the Philadelphia Sports Writers Association Award as the Most Courageous Athlete in America; Mrs. Rosalyn Carter will host a White House reception for her; she'll throw out the first pitch to open the baseball season for the Los Angeles Dodgers and the Atlanta Braves.

"Kathy also will become the subject of a best-selling book and a made-for-television movie viewed by millions." I never could have conceived it. It's far beyond anything I'd dream or ask for. But it all happened.

Less dramatic, less spectacular, but far more important and lasting, we four Millers individually began to believe the words Kathy so often spoke, or wrote in her journal: WITH THE LORD'S HELP, I'M GONNA WIN!

Just as Kathy's terribly broken body, mind, and emotions have been rebuilt, every injured relationship within our family has been renewed. We're still working on it. And as we travel together on business or fun, we observe far more than we once did. We see hurting families, fathers and sons who don't speak, mothers and daughters in open competition. We see the hurt in their eyes and want to tell them, "With the Lord's help, you can win."

So many mothers, so many teenage girl friends, urged Barbara and Kathy to write this book. The story is quite personal and close to our hearts. It's a story for people like us, those who seem to have everything, yet don't always know how to show love or ask for it.

I want Barb and Kathy to share what God did for them. It's their inning. As for Larry Don and myself, our miracle's still in process.

An unforgettable thing happened the evening Kathy received the International Award for Valour in Sport in London on February 15, 1978. We sat at the head table near Russia's ambassador to England. He and I attempted dinner conversation, but found it forced and stilted. How could we really talk, when we could not agree on religion, politics, government, economics, or anything else important?

Then they announced Kathy as winner, taking several minutes to tell how she fought her way back from a fifty-pound vegetable. This was a very emotional time. People all around us were sniffling. As I reached for my handkerchief, I happened to glance at the stolid Russian ambassador, and saw he was shedding big tears, just like me.

I thought, *Isn't this incredible?* Here we were, a Russian and an American, poles apart on so many issues, and yet, at that moment, sharing our mutual feelings, not as an American and a Russian, but as two fathers who cared deeply for their children.

I'll always remember that moment. Even though our country's traditions affect our attitudes on matters that place us in opposition to other countries, we all share a common bond in our love for our children. To that extent, we are one large family of man who share a common desire for our children to prosper and succeed.

God wants that, too. This book says it's never too late for parent and child, husband and wife, to rebuild. We four Millers, formerly so emotionally bankrupt, can attest to that. With all our hearts we urge you to give God a chance. We know from experience that through the power of His love you can say with us:

With the Lord's help, we're gonna win!

LARRY MILLER

The four Millers, Larry, Kathy, Barbara, and Larry Don, on one of their happiest family days: Kathy's high-school graduation, May 1981.

Come out,
　　Come out
wherever you are!

When you're hurting,
　　you withdraw.
That's Satan's call,
　　to go within.
God's call is
　　to exodus!

　　The Reverend Richard Rohr, O.F.M.

That which we have seen and heard declare we unto
you, that ye also may have fellowship with us: and
truly our fellowship is with the Father, and with his
Son Jesus Christ. And these things write we unto you,
that your joy may be full.

　　1 John 1:3, 4

1

Tears, Turmoil, and Truth

I recall the day so clearly—one of those early autumn days that seems to burn like a flame, the sort of blue-and-gold afternoon Scottsdale, Arizona, feasts on each October. As I drove down a street in my neighborhood, alone and carefree, I savored the trees, the colors, the thin, cool air.

Abruptly, from nowhere, for no reason I could understand, gushes of tears began pouring down my face. I was not just crying, but weeping with noisy abandon: great, gusty sobs, the kind that threaten to tear the very lining of your stomach loose. I steered my car to the curb and parked it, by now overwhelmingly broken and totally mystified. *What was happening to me?*

I didn't want to cry. After eighteen months of sheer miracle, why cry now? Larry had wept sometimes following Kathy's tragedy; had cried aloud in his grief and frustration. I understood, since at that time he really did not know God personally; I did, and God had kept me strong, had given me a supernatural faith.

Had it not been enough, those first days, that Kathy actually lived? How could I weep then, when we were living on hope? And if I hadn't cried during those first desperate days, surely tears now would be an affront to God. He had shown us victory after victory. I needed to praise Him, not break down like this. Why, we were writing a book while the miracles were fresh in our minds. . . .

The wrenching weeping only worsened. Sure we were tired, bone-tired. Sure the bills continued to mount. And of course, Larry, Larry Don, and I stayed strung out—*but we were making it.*

Above all, I had to stay spiritually strong. *Had* to, because I was the only one. And anyway, He was my strength—had been all this time, hour by hour—and tears couldn't accomplish one single thing, certainly not now, after the fact.

Barbara Miller normally was not a weeper. I'd always been self-controlled and decisive. I considered myself a strong person, someone able to handle emergencies well. Now, however, I found myself way out of control, literally torn out of my frame. I couldn't stop crying, couldn't stop shaking, couldn't stop the convulsive sobs that sounded so horribly loud on that quiet suburban street.

At last the shuddering crying stopped, and I slumped against the steering wheel, too exhausted to move. "Lord, what's happening to me?" I whispered. "What in the *world* is wrong?"

It's the kind of question He sometimes answers very quickly. Immediately, a long-forgotten scene invaded my memory—a vivid flashback to a day three weeks prior to Kathy's near-fatal accident in this same neighborhood. I was not recalling the accident itself, but an afternoon three weeks earlier, in this very location, at this same time of day. Now the memory resounded against my brain as clear as a bell. It appalled me.

That day I'd waited impatiently for Kathy's return from school, for we had a dental appointment and needed to hurry. Watching from our front door, I saw Kathy and her friend dawdle toward the intersection a block away—and then walk right past our street. That did it! I dashed to my car, drove up to the girls, and told them to jump in right now.

Something felt odd. As the girls quickly scrambled into the car, I noticed fear and apprehension on their faces. They said nothing, simply looked relieved to see me. When we pulled into traffic, an automobile ahead of us slowed, pulled alongside, and the woman driver indicated she wanted to speak to me. I pulled over. She parked her car ahead of mine and quickly walked back to us—a brisk, tailored, businesswoman, probably driving home from work, I figured.

She addressed Kathy's friend first. "Young lady," she said in a cool, level tone, "I don't know who you are, but I want you to know one thing. That word means a female dog. Remember that the next time you use it."

I practically went into shock, but managed to speak. "This is our friend," I said, indicating the mute teenager in the backseat. "The girl beside me is my daughter, Kathy."

At that, the lady looked straight into Kathy's eyes. "And as for you, young lady," she continued, *"you almost made me the victim of your demise!"*

The woman's controlled yet obvious anger, the girls' unusual behavior, aroused a deep, instinctive wariness in me. The rest of the story took but a moment—an uncomfortable moment for each of us. The girls had been lollygagging along the street, she told me, and Kathy had stepped out without looking. She might have gone directly into the path of the woman's car, had the driver been not quite so alert.

To make matters worse, it seemed the shaken woman served as head nurse for the county hospital's neurological

ward. She constantly came into contact with tragically damaged kids, kids who'd been lively and intelligent, yet one
careless mistake left them dead—or even worse than dead—
inert, unresponsive humans whose brains could never re-
cover normalcy. "I see this all the time," she told Kathy.
"You could have caused me to suffer forever for what I did
to you—and I couldn't have prevented it!"

I cried harder now, revolted by my memory of the scene's
painful, clear-cut implications. *God, how could I have
blocked out that episode so completely?*

Now it hit me hard, each detail stinging like a whip
against my raw nerves. Every time I tried to refresh my
tear-blotched face, some new realization would occur to me,
and fresh tears would ruin whatever repairs I'd been able to
make.

God warned us, I realized. *God had warned us. Dear God,
she did it just three weeks later—got hit by a car, and from
that day to this the anguish, the hopes, the suffering of us
all.* . . .

I forced my unwilling mind to travel back, to recollect the
rest of the story. What became of that woman? Why nothing, I realized with chagrin—nothing at all. I had *meant* to
drop by her office, take her some flowers, and thank her for
what she did.

But I never bought those flowers, never thanked the angry
lady—the frightened woman whose name I had forgotten.
The lady who'd surely been an angel, unaware.

I believe God arranged that confrontation with reality for
Barbara Miller that afternoon. He was preparing me to understand some hard things, to face truths He knew would set
me free.

Today I'm certain that totally unexpected, coming-un-glued experience signaled an important step toward further healing God meant to schedule for me many months later. That day, however, I simply saw myself as a woman who had, by the grace of God, survived some very tough times. I also perceived myself as the most fortunate among all moth-ers, a woman given a second chance with a beloved daugh-ter God had so mercifully spared from death or permanent brain damage.

At that time I saw us Millers as such an all 'round, typical American family: handsome, successful father; energetic, devoted mother; bright, talented son, and a winner of a daughter. Sure we had problems—typical growing pains. Doesn't everyone?

We were *survivors.* I'd learned that a high percentage of all families who sustain a physical, emotional, financial, and spiritual trauma as serious as ours inevitably will split up. I'd vowed that would not happen to us. I'd fight that out-come with every prayer, every effort, every fiber of my body.

Later (in fact a year and one-half later), as God brought me face to face with truths I longed to deny, I would recog-nize that rendevous with God beside that curbstone as a divine appointment. I'd realize at that later time that the Millers indeed *were* a typical American family: part of the 95 percent which are out of order. I'd even begin to accept that it was not Kathy's accident that had produced such overwhelming stress within our family, but that our stress-filled family might have produced in her a near-fatal care-lessness.

In time, God would show us those and other even more devastating truths. That day, however, I certainly didn't consider the Miller family nonfunctional. We loved one another deeply and strongly. We're close, caring, affectionate people, a family willing to invest heavily in one another. Possibly we would have termed ourselves above average in those ways.

Later we'd face the truth—that for some time the Millers had been on a collision course. We *were* out of order. Never had we been truly functional, with God at the family's head, the husband under God, the wife under her husband, and the children reared and protected by all three.

I remained ignorant of all that, that gorgeous autumn afternoon in Scottsdale. As I pulled away from the curb, exhausted, as my car crept down the dreamy, golden street, I didn't know there'd be a day when I'd actually thank God for triggering that embarrassing, inexplicable, public crying jag!

2

My Problem, His Potential

The good news is, God wants to bring the sort of turmoil I just described into a clear, understandable perspective. My deep desire to write this book stems from a priceless discovery: *understanding the basis for good relationships is not all that obscure and difficult.*

With God's help, you and I can learn how to change even a desperately poor relationship into something vital, dynamic and good. Right now, think of the single worst person-related problem in your life. Visualize him or her, then imagine this: *your relationship to that individual can begin this moment to change from death into life.*

How can I state that so confidently? Because I can look back and marvel at what God began in Barbara Miller one Monday afternoon in Scottsdale, Arizona—the day our daughter's body and mind seemed close to extinction. Larry and I might have described that day as the most heartbreaking time of our lives. Yet today, even Larry Don and Kathy recognize that "accident" as a divine catalyst for much-needed change in each of us.

Naturally, at a time like that, most of us find it almost impossible to see God's redemptive power at work. Larry says he'd look at Kathy's broken little body and think *hopeless, tragic waste,* and the like. As a Christian, I *tried* not to limit God. It seemed imperative that I try hard to believe. As we shared in our book *Kathy,* God was faithful from the first to reward each of my tiniest exercises in faith so I grew—and later my husband grew—into a sure knowledge that . . . "all things work together for good to them that love God, to them who are the called according to his purpose" (Romans 8:28).

Of course, a medical emergency like ours calls forth every ounce of a family's reserves. You call on God with every prayer you know how to pray. It took us much longer, I confess, to understand how much God also yearns to heal the invisible, unspoken *inner* brokenness in His children. A crippled relationship, a failing marriage, inability to trust— we should have flung ourselves on God for those things with the same all-out faith, hope, and total effort we exerted toward Kathy's obvious needs.

Why is that so hard to do? For one thing, Larry and I believe most of us look at our problems exactly backwards. Ordinarily we can't picture much positive potential in the everyday hassles you and I face: stubborn, frightened, aging parents; wayward offspring; alcoholism; a pregnant teenager; drug abuse; divorce; parent-child rebellion; the whole catalog of hurt.

Can you believe God sees such things as opportunities? Well, join the club. We didn't see things that way either! Today, however, Larry likes to quote Dr. Norman Vincent Peale's unforgettable thought: "Thank God for your problems. They mean you're alive. People in cemeteries don't have any problems whatever, but all the rest of us do!"

As Larry paraphrases it, "Thank God for your kid who's smoking grass. He's still alive. You still have a chance with him. There's still hope." Then he describes Kathy's room, and how before her accident he was always on her back about keeping it in order. Then she was in a ten-and-a-half-week coma, and the room was so clean, neat, and sterile. "I prayed that God would give me the privilege of seeing her bed unmade, pillows tossed in the corner, clothes dumped in a chair," he said. "That represented life. Someone had lived in that room. It haunted me to see it so quiet."

Of course it's not easy (certainly not automatic) to see real potential within our problems. Our family have had to face some heavy stuff, still face parts of it, and believe we have had experiences worth sharing. Above all, we *know* God's power to heal, renew, and restore each person and each relationship, from the ground up.

The first thing Barbara Miller had to realize was that He wanted to begin with *me*. And to my astonishment, God began working in the rather wrinkled area of my low self-worth!

Now, I wouldn't have seen it that way. After all, at the time of Kathy's accident I had been an active, seeking, growing Christian for five years. Early on, I'd been fortunate to discover a life-changing Christian book entitled *Woman: Aware and Choosing*, by Betty J. Coble. That book had a real impact on my life, and I wound up teaching courses from it. I felt I'd found a real handle for my personal needs as a woman, a wife, and a Christian.

Also, I'd always come across as the sort of peppy, enthusiastic personality who manages to succeed at most of the things she tries to do. I definitely would have told you I possessed a healthy self-image!

Not only did that self-diagnosis prove faulty, however, but from today's vantage point, I'd state that *every relationship problem that exists contains some element of deficient self-worth.*

In my own case, since I had Christ at the center of my life, since I sincerely sought to please Him and build my life around Him, and since I was such an optimist by nature, I'd never have dreamed that down deep, I didn't like myself very well. Consequently, I couldn't begin to love myself in any meaningful way, nor did I realize that I loved others in the same, flawed way I perceived myself.

How did God reveal those truths to me? Much of it came through Kathy. Simplistically stated, as I attempted to help teach and train my thirteen-year-old "baby" anew, I sought to instill in her nothing but positive, faith-filled attitudes. Hour by hour, I drilled Kathy on her value to God and to each of us. I told her she was smart, brave, pretty, a real winner. In my unceasing efforts to feed her the most "vitamin-packed" spiritual, mental, and emotional food, I read Scripture passages; prayed with her; did all in my power to convince her at the core of her being that she is irreplaceably valuable, infinitely precious, in the sight of God.

Somehow, sometime, during all of this, those truths began to slip into my own spirit. You see, not only the daughter, but to an even greater extent, the mother needed to be transformed by the renewing of her mind!

Meanwhile, as we prepared to write this book, Kathy and I had to divert our efforts, so I could go to California and help my mother, Doris Barlow, move into a nursing home. That's a difficult chore at best, but particularly so for me, since Mother and I never had attained anything like an ideal relationship. She loved me. I loved her. Why had that deep, fierce love so often caused each of us such pain?

I'd always thought we simply were too much alike. That answer really doesn't make sense, but it'll have to do. Now since the Lord had brought me a way in relating first to

Kathy, then Larry Don, and finally to the courage to believe in Him to restore Larry and me to that love that began during our college days—now, at last, I had the courage to tackle Mother. She was still a tiger (my two sisters and our brother agreed, all of us aware of our mom's spirited personality).

I flew to California with high resolve (and a bit of trepidation), to move Mom into a nursing home. For two days I drove from one nursing home to the next, interviewing directors and touring their facilities, trying to decide where to place Mom. Then I prayed, and it came clear that a woman who had been so independent throughout her life ought to be allowed the privilege of choosing her new surroundings.

The next day I loaded Mom's oxygen tank and wheelchair into the car and, with the help of a friend and Mom's nurse, away we went to select her new home. It was a difficult move which brought some of the old antagonisms straight to the surface—in fact, some of the old Barbara Miller threatened to return, too! But then . . . the miracle happened.

At first I didn't recognize it. It took flying back to Scottsdale, to my men and to Kathy, for me to regroup and realize the most exciting fact in the world. *My mother and I had begun a fundamental healing to our relationship.* She was not too old. I was not too stuck in the same old groove. We were not manipulating one another in the old, hurtful ways. I was acting the part of a grown woman, not a wheedling child. Praise the Lord!

Here's the lasting part—the eternal benefit. Mother lived in that nursing home for a total of less than twelve weeks. Then, suddenly and beautifully, she went to be with the Lord.

Before she left, God allowed us plenty of time for all she and I needed to do. He gave us adequate, complete, and thorough woman-to-woman communication. Not only did that provide me with every key I needed for understanding my own early life, but God also enabled me to understand my proud, fierce, beautiful little mother's basic ego needs and how they had affected first her, then me, then my daughter.

No, I am not a professional psychologist. I simply say to you that the Spirit of God did the work Mother and I needed individually and between us, and He did it perfectly. Today my mother no longer sees "through a glass, darkly" (1 Corinthians 13:12). It excites me that Doris Barlow, my mother and my friend, for some time now has enjoyed perfect and total life with the Giver of Life.

Before she left, God worked through Mom to help me understand and overcome some of the rips in the fabric of my personalilty. No longer do I have to blame my mother for those torn places in me. What's more, now I can love myself, and I understand how important it is to God for me to love Barbara Miller, His child.

Godly self-love is the starting place, where bad relationships are concerned. Kathy has some things to say about loving yourself, which I really wish I'd known at her age.

Kathy and I pray, as you read our story, that God will show you exactly how to begin loving, not only that difficult other person, but yourself as well!

3

The Neatest Lady I Know

Wow! What a fantastic day this is!

Was just browsing through some of my journals, what I call my *feelin'* books, to help me remember some points I want to be sure to include here. Couldn't help but smile to see that almost every single time I had begun just as I did this chapter—that it's a *fabulous* day. Some days are bummers, but very few.

Life's exciting. Maybe that's why I've kept some sort of diary, usually a beat-up spiral notebook, ever since I can remember. The ones from the early days of my rehabilitation are something else. I had to learn to write left-handed, since the brain damage affected my right hand, but the Lord helped me learn to write again. He also gave me plenty to say. Praise the Lord!

When Mom and I decided to write about mother-daughter relationships (at least from our experience of building that relationship for a *second* time as I made my comeback), we thought we'd have an awful lot to share. After all, we've been privileged to speak in churches, meetings, business conventions, women's groups, on national television, and one-on-one testimony for five years now. We've met literally thousands of mothers and daughters all over America, and wherever else we've traveled, and it's sad how many of them aren't making it.

33

But we didn't know the *half* of it! We started praying about our book, wanting to share in written form what God has done for us, hoping we could get it together. As Mom kept saying after every meeting where we spoke, "It's their eyes—those sad eyes—those women who wish they were free to love their daughters openly, as I love you—those beautiful young girls, so hostile to their mothers, so unhappy. . . ."

I saw those eyes, too, and I urged Mom, "Let's try to write some of our experiences." You see, the way our family was heading, had it not been for my accident, I wonder where we'd all be today.

Of course I'm *not* saying it takes a disastrous accident for God to turn people around. What I am saying, in our case, is that God used the effects of my injuries in His redemptive way. My mother had to help reprogram my mind from the word *go.* She literally had the rare privilege of raising me from babyhood *twice!*

For the record, she's always been a great mother. We were close and loving, and great friends; but also for the record, I was a typical, sometimes rebellious thirteen-year-old. Oh, sweet on the outside, maybe, and not inclined to make many waves, but inside Kathy Miller at the time of the accident a storm was brewin'. While I was in a coma, Mom and Dad found some of my journals and dipped in here and there, only to discover a few things they didn't enjoy reading. *Inside,* I wasn't exactly the happy-go-lucky kid they thought I was!

That's not fatal, of course. Most kids go through stages like that, at least all the ones I knew. I was about average, I'd say.

However, the second time Mom "raised" me from babyhood, there was a major difference in the whole picture. Here I was, fifty-five pounds, unable to walk, talk, or even think (so far as anyone really could tell), with nobody encouraging my mother to expect much better out of me.

The difference, I know you guessed, is our Lord Jesus Christ. Mom knew that with His help, I was going to win. She taught me that every way she knew how, because she believed with all her heart that it was true.

And when you train up a "baby" in the way she should go, it takes the hard edges off the relationship. People sometimes ask me if Mom and I love each other the way we do (she's my best friend, for sure!) because I had to depend on her for literally everything.

No, I love Mom this way because the Lord started us off a second time—only this time loving the way He intends. After all, I'm not dependent on her now. I don't love her because I need her, I love her because she's about the neatest lady I know. I'm glad I've got a lot of her traits, and that I look like her. I'm glad I have Mom around as my model. The Bible says the older women should teach the younger women (Titus 2:3–5), and she teaches me by example lots of things I really need to know.

My mother stays enthusiastic, always ready to get in there and work. She's tremendously versatile and well organized, like the godly woman in Proverbs 31. Maybe the best thing she's got going for her, though: she has an understanding heart!

I wish you could meet this woman. She's a good wife and mother, puts God first and my dad and us second, and really believes in marriage. We talk a lot about marriage, and how I can prepare for it. (I want to write a chapter about that later.) To sum it up, my mother is my prayer partner, my business partner and my friend. We're adults together now, and it's great.

Just five years ago, a severely injured Kathryn Suzanne Miller had to be carried or wheeled out to the patio to lie in the sun or practice walking in the pool, where the water helped my legs learn to function. Those mornings I remember how Mom went about teaching me to talk.

There we'd be, stretched out in the sun, taking in those tanning rays, and she'd have a copy of *Vogue* magazine for us to browse through. Though I could hardly communicate, Mom would enthusiastically point out the various fashion outfits, turning pages, making me look at this dress or that pair of shoes, making me focus my eyes—and my brain.

Despite everything, she'd coax me to talk. I might say something like, "I like the dress, but not the helmet."

"Helmet, Kathy?" she'd ask. "Think. Think of the word. What is it we wear on our heads?"

I'd struggle and struggle, like trying to open a locked door without a key, and sometimes anger and frustration got the best of me. She'd let me work for a moment, then Mom would say, "Hat, Kathy. *H-A-T.* She has a hat on her head."

I'd repeat the word several times, and then something amazing would happen. It seemed that when I learned a new word, often the Lord would open doors in my mind, and a whole block of new words would come tumbling back into my memory. Then Mom and I, and later Dad and Larry Don, would get so excited!

It was such a wonderful process. There was so awfully much to relearn, but Mom chose to teach me with fun methods as much as possible. We got into fashion together and made something of a study of it, mostly as a way to help me think and talk. Later, when I could go out in public, Mom would take me to department stores, and we'd study the different outfits, talking over together which we liked, which we disliked, and why.

I know the Lord had a hand in all that, because in 1980, Mom and a terrific writer named Charles Paul Conn wrote a book entitled *Kathy*. Then the traveling started—all over the United States and beyond, national television programs; the White House; more different doors opening than anybody could dream of.

Isn't it great we'd gotten into fashion? Suddenly we had to get some workable traveling clothes, because we really hit the road to tell people about the goodness of the Lord.

More important than clothes, though, we had to have a workable *relationship*, because traveling, public appearances, television, all that stuff can create *stress*. You better believe Satan would like to get the best of two people in that situation!

Praise the Lord, Mom and I have traveled many thousands of miles together. It has been one of the best experiences any girl could have with her mother. We've had mountaintop moments, plus certain challenges you wouldn't believe. We've had glamour hotels and late-hour waiting in airports. We've been tired and homesick at times, but mostly we've felt like two of the world's most fortunate women.

You see, the Lord opened doors for Mom and me *together*. It won't always be this way, because in a few years I'll probably be married and making a home of my own. Meantime I want to say to every teenage girl in the world, take time right now and begin making friends with your mother. Put all that anger and guilt and unhappiness away, and start all over with her.

Sure you can do it! The Lord will help you, but you need to be the one to make the first move. We're going to talk about some ways to do that, some practical ways to begin. You see, though I don't know you face to face, I do know one thing about you. Down deep, you desperately want to love your mother and for her to love you.

Praise God, it can happen! If God did it for Mom and me, He'll do it for you!

4
Love and Marriage

My mother picked out my husband. (At least, that's what we always jokingly said.) She and I were in fine fettle the day we met him, all gussied up for my first day at the University of Kansas. It was just a thirty-two-mile drive from home to school, so I got to handle Dad's sharp new car. Since Dad worked as head of quality control for General Motors, we always drove new cars.

I felt nervous, excited, and high-strung that day—eighteen years old, my first time away from home, and driving a vehicle that was new to me. As I drove up to what would become my new home, I felt embarrassed to see a long, solid line of young men. Imagine how disconcerting that would be—all those young men *looking* at you.

Among that group was my future husband. Larry was a junior that year (an older man), there supposedly to supervise the others. They were a pledge class, it turned out, and their job was to welcome and help the newcomers.

I'd never been a great one for parallel parking, at that point, and flustered as I was, I knew I couldn't maneuver into the tiny parking space we spied. Typically, Mom took over. Here I was with this delightful, tiny, gutsy little lady who talked with her hands a lot. Now she was motioning to Larry and saying to me, "Oh, get that big handsome one— see the big one over there?—to help you."

Larry loped over, responding to Mother's vigorous waves, and I mumbled something to him about my having difficulty parking my car. Larry took over immediately, but I'm a short woman, and he's a tall man, and he forgot to push the front seat back. My first good look at Larry was with his knees up around his chin, as he parked my dad's car for me. He then took my things to my room, introduced himself to my mother and me, and was gone.

I often saw Larry Miller around the campus. He'd pop up almost everywhere I went, and he usually made it a point to speak to me. Months after our first meeting I learned his fraternity-house rules forbade him to ask me for a date if I were dating another man from that house, so it was not until after I'd been out of school sick for a couple of weeks that spring that he became eligible to ask me out!

Our friendship took off from there, blossoming very quickly into romance. After all, Larry Miller personified all the traits I most admired in a man. He was an outstanding scholar and athlete, ambitious, hardworking, self-disciplined, and a real "take-charge guy." He knew who he was and what he wanted. I not only loved him, but admired him in every way. All those solid character traits, combined with a terrific personality and exceptionally good looks—I knew this guy was somebody special!

By May, we were talking marriage, and were sort of unofficially engaged when we parted for the summer—he to play baseball, me to find a job.

That fall Larry returned to school, and Barbara remained home as part of the work force. I'd landed a job at an exclusive boutique to earn money for my wedding gown and the beautiful trousseau I was collecting.

Our plans seemed fantastically exciting. Larry visited us

most weekends, usually bedding down on a bed in the basement. I loved watching him get to know Dad and Mom, my brother, and two sisters. He fit into our family so easily. I felt so happy, so much in love!

Looking back, I realize just how happy and relieved Mom felt, having me close by at that particular time. She adored Larry and thought I was the luckiest girl she knew, to find a fine young man like him. But from this perspective, I realize she couldn't have been comfortable had I returned to school that year. She feared the possibility of a physical intimacy between Larry and me and wanted to keep me under her wing—so the tension mounted.

In fact, the closer the wedding date approached, the more Mom complained about Larry's regular weekend visits in our home. About six weeks before the wedding, she and I were really strung out. She criticized every little thing I did, and seemed suddenly antagonistic toward Larry for no reason at all.

"Why should you do his laundry?" she'd ask me. "It's almost like he's living with us. What in the world do the neighbors think about you?"

Mother always was highly verbal. When she got disturbed, she'd often be quite unkind with her tongue, so those weeks found us at sword's point. Just when I wanted to savor the greatest happiness, security, and love I'd ever felt in my life, she and I would erupt. She insisted that Larry should stay at a motel, that it should not look as though he were living with us, lest people should think I were not a nice girl. . . .

The more she ranted, the more she raised her voice in these discussions, the quieter and more reasonable I would become. Mother and I were arguing about where Larry stayed. I made the point that it was far more important that he feel wanted and welcome, that he have a chance to grow to love my family, than it was for us to worry about what our neighbors might think.

I simply didn't realize that the issue over which we argued had no bearing on what was going on within my mother at that time. I was too young and inexperienced to understand the mixed emotions within her. On the one hand, she loved this young man almost to the point of worship. Conversely, he seemed—suddenly—almost like a threat. He was so smart, handsome, and sweet—and about to take her oldest daughter from her.

Before Larry entered my life, my mom always had a loving control over me. Now I was offering that control over my life into Larry's hands—and my mom wasn't ready for that. So the tensions in our home continued to mount as the wedding date approached, with each of the principals handling those tensions in his or her typical fashion. Mom raged. I tried to placate her. Dad disappeared, often with a drink in his hand.

Just past my nineteenth birthday, just about to become married to Mr. Wonderful, enjoying a closet full of bridal finery I'd earned myself, and dreaming of living happily ever after, why would an optimistic girl like me let Mother's little flaps create any undue concern?

Joyful and starry-eyed, I found it easy enough to ignore Mom's outbursts and get on with my future. She loved me deeply, as I did her. But my temperament was quite different from hers. When Barbara Barlow Miller established *her* home, there would be *no* raised voices, I decided.

Ten months after our rapturous wedding, Larry and I welcomed little Larry Don into our lives. Even though I was just twenty years old, I felt ecstatic. Larry, after all, was twenty-four and took added responsibility well in stride. Both of us were thrilled with our bright, beautiful baby son. I loved my life; loved the role of Mrs. Larry Miller; thoroughly enjoyed being the wife of a professional baseball player. Everything was going great.

A year or so later, however, we experienced an unexplainable episode, one I didn't know how to handle. By then Larry had been called into military service, and we were stationed at Fort Sill, near Lawton, Oklahoma. Army life, in fact, was a whole different ball game, but Larry, Larry Don, and I were trying hard to adapt. The hardest thing for me, however, was that I was having letters I'd written to my mother returned, stamped NOT AT THIS ADDRESS.

I began phoning home, but my sisters would answer and tell me Mom didn't want to speak to me. The times Mom did answer, she hung up on me. That's very painful, that sort of rejection. Worst of all, I had no idea what was wrong. After several weeks of this mystifying stuff, my emotions had begun to take a beating.

"Something's wrong, Barbara. You need to go home and take care of the situation," Larry advised. His kindness and concern brought a lump to my throat, and a rush of homesickness, as I thought of Dad and Mom, and the others. I took the baby and went, without notifying Mom or anyone else.

Mom and I stayed up all night, talking. What came forth from her was attack after attack after attack. A lot of it concerned Larry, and hurt me a lot.

Now at that time I did not know Jesus Christ, but I did believe in God and went to church every Sunday. Now I breathed a silent prayer and asked Him to help me hang in

there, and to keep my tongue quiet. He did help me, and I
could hear the hurtful things Mother said without responding in an inflammatory way. I also could realize that she was
not speaking truth, but simply had a tremendous need to air
those pent-up, hostile feelings.

After literally a full night of nonstop verbiage, at last I
had the sense to hug Mom and say, "I see you're afraid you
have lost me, and that I don't love you anymore. You know
someone has come into my life, and I love him so very
much—and he *is* so important to me—but Mom, he can't
take away any of the love I've always felt for you."

I also recall saying, "Mother, it would seem to me, knowing the unhappiness you've experienced with Dad, that
you'd be overjoyed to see Larry and me building a strong,
happy family. Instead, what I'm seeing is envy."

We tried hard to communicate that long, difficult night.
After we worked through some of it, I clearly saw a tremendous need in my mother, not only to be reassured that I
loved her, but to hear me say it with words. We ended with
hugs, tears, *I love you*s, and my mother's invariable heartfelt
plea: "Will you forgive me?"

Of course I did. I'd grown up with a superemotional,
high-strung mother who could be vicious with her mouth. I
never knew when some innocent remark of mine might pro-
voke her fury, and I'd find myself fending off a barrage of
hurtful words: "You're fat . . . you're frumpy . . . you're un-
intelligent . . . I hate you. . . ."

Then—equally suddenly, bewilderingly—she'd exhibit
the utmost remorse, hugging and kissing me, assuring me
that she loved me and didn't mean any of the things she'd

said. I was used to that pattern. I somehow understood that she couldn't help it; it's just the way she was.

I also knew my mother loved me, just as I loved and admired much about her, but I feared those attacks. I feared what they did to me. I worked hard at countering them by keeping a cool, quiet, almost nonemotional manner of speaking.

Interestingly enough, I never told Larry the truth about that visit home. I chose not to. I explained to him that I'd been bad about not writing to Mom, or phoning, and she needed reassurance from me. In essence, that was the truth, but you notice I protected Larry from knowing about Mom's attacks on him. I was afraid he wouldn't understand, that the love between them might be broken.

Mother never attacked my husband again. However, from time to time she became ill. Her sicknesses always seemed sudden, unexplainable and serious. A pattern developed wherein I would go to her, take care of her, and give her a lot of attention.

It took some fifteen years for me to understand that indeed there *was* a pattern, one which became set some fifteen years ago when my father died of a heart attack. He and mother had long been unhappy, due to his alcoholism, she said, and just prior to his unexpected death, Mom told me she just couldn't take living with an alcoholic any longer. She wanted a divorce.

Then he died, and she became the totally inconsolable widow. On the surface that seemed rank hypocrisy, yet we could see she truly did miss him. Her pattern of life by then had become almost total conflict. The conflict seemed worth it to her, because after all the work and all the pain came the exquisite pleasure of making up—the release of tears—the reassurance that we all loved her.

In truth, Mom really did love my father. The battles, the perpetual conflict, the family arguments I always so dreaded, none of that disguised the fact that she really loved this alcoholic and often inadequate man. She missed him, and she missed the conflict. Dad was our buffer zone, the one who, when the battle was over, reassured her, built her up, told her she was loved.

After Dad died, Mom simply transferred her battles to us kids and various other friends and family members. Almost without exception, when she loved someone, she inevitably would drive him from her. Her behavior in this respect remained consistent throughout her life.

So Mom lived out her greatest fear, that of growing lonely, ill, and alone. Yet during these past two years God has given me a clear view of my mother, an understanding not threatened by all that happened between us in the past.

How did He help me see Mom more clearly? By giving me a better understanding of myself. As I asked Him, *Who am I?* I began also to ask, *Who is Mom? Who is that person with whom I lived all those years?*

Before, when I hardly knew myself, all I consciously "saw" in Mom were the things I didn't like. But as I came to love and understand myself, I began to see so many things about my mother that I was proud to inherit from her.

What's more, God also produced in me an amazing love and acceptance for this remarkable woman who, despite a flawed life, nevertheless did love us, did exemplify numerous strong traits I'm glad to inherit, and did involve herself in life right up to her last breath.

Like all the rest of us, my mom was a mixed bag of traits,

habits, emotions, behavior, gifts, and talents. I learned to look at the entire package. Because of her, I learned to love and not to fear.

Because of that, I was able to learn much about myself, the Barbara Barlow Miller who is so much like Doris Barlow; the Barbara Barlow who married young and left home and all its conflicts. In fact, I'm still learning a lot about the girl I was, the one so naïve as to believe you really can grow up, leave home, and take none of the problems with you.

Who is Barbara Miller? For part of an answer to that, look back to Doris Barlow. And who was Doris Barlow? Well, you'd have to look back to Grandma Jennings. . . .

Mother to daughter to granddaughter, and so on—we're a continuum. Whether we look forward or back, we spring one from another, nor can any of us truly understand ourselves, apart from understanding those other women who helped to shape us.

Who are you? Like it or not, you must look to your mother for part of the answer, and then to her mother—and then, if you have been blessed with a daughter, you'll catch a glimpse or even a portrait of your true self when you see her.

It's a great mystery. I came to see that I couldn't simply turn my back on my mother, ignore the things about her I couldn't understand, move away to where she could not affect me. In truth, I took her with me, because I am part Doris. The day came when I needed to know my Self, and I realized I'd have to seek out my mother.

Then came the miracle, for only through loving and accepting my Self—*all of myself*—could I begin to love and accept my mother.

An impossible challenge, you say? Not really. God's garden of people includes plenty of offbeat, even "impossible" characters—maybe like me or even you! Whether they're offbeat or not, His Word tells us: "Honour thy father and thy mother: that thy days may be long upon the land which the Lord thy God giveth thee" (Exodus 20:12).

Long life. It's easy to see honor, acceptance, and understanding as keys to contentment, inner peace, and hence, long life. Experts verify that the stress, tensions, and simple conflicts that enter our lives so early—and so often begin in our childhood homes—lead to disease, pain, and even death. These days, even babies experience ulcers; kindergarten children consume tranquilizers.

As a pretty, wide-eyed nineteen-year-old, eager to enter into the most wondrous new relationship my heart could imagine, I knew very little about myself. I felt certain I wanted to move out from my parents' home, graduate from my role as Barbara Barlow, eldest daughter, and assume a newer, headier role. I would become Mrs. Larry Miller; that's all that mattered to me at that time.

Love and marriage. Barbara Barlow, age nineteen, wanted those above anything else in life. For me, however, that phrase should read *marriage and love.* For it was the role of Mrs. Larry Miller that within ten years brought Barbara Miller to the end of the "role" and into a search for her Self.

Each woman has her own unique starting point. For me, a "perfect" marriage eventually brought me face to face with an interior emptiness that forced me into growth and change.

Five years later, Kathy Miller had to start over too. Her horrible accident wiped out her predictable role as typical teenager, Daddy's girl, and family pet. The all-American stereotypes were removed. She found herself forced into self-confrontation very early. This brought forth the strengths that will undergird her entire womanhood.

For me, it was *marriage and love.* For Kathy, I believe it can be *love and marriage,* for I believe her marriage will find her ready to love. She began her search for her Self very early. She knows and accepts that Self in a way her mother might envy.

Our daughters can teach us a lot. Praise God, because of Kathy, I also had to grow up fast. It was through her, and later through our son, Larry Don, that I encountered growth, change, and insights, which ultimately led me into new freedom—freedom for a deeply thrilling, mature marriage.

Kathy

5
"New" Mother, "New" Daughter

"Old things have passed away. . . ." *Hallelujah!*

I used to see my mother as . . . my mother. She was a typical mother, I thought, always doubting, often critical, and judging me. I had to have my defenses up, for sure.

Yet, we were close. Mom was proud of me, and I knew her critical attitudes had a purpose. She wanted me to turn out right. I knew she loved me, and I took it for granted that she was supposed to do all that stuff that mothers do—the car pools, costumes, birthday parties, new dresses, helping with homework—all that.

Mom always let me bring my friends home. When I was seven, and it was time for her to teach me to cook, she let me invite several friends and actually had a little cooking school for us that summer. We loved it.

Yep, I'd have said my mother was better than averge. We had a good family, but it was as though each one of us worried about "me, myself, and I." We were all busy working on good things, but just for *ourselves*. We weren't quick, when someone else had a problem or a trial, to get in and help him with it. I know I was wrapped up in myself!

I had a lot of girl friends, and they all related to their mothers in pretty much the same way. I can't remember ever having a friend who felt about her mother the way I now

51

feel about mine. As little girls go, I guess you'd say I was about average.

Then came my accident. I remember a few things about it: remember waking up after ten and one-half weeks in a coma, unable to communicate. I thought they had put me into a jail; I didn't know where I was or what was wrong with me. It was horrible.

When I first woke up, I remember looking out my window and seeing a church steeple—the Catholic church across the street from the hospital. Then I saw my mother: Mom was the *first* person I saw. Later, she was the first person I called by name.

I remember my mother very clearly at that time. She was really loving. She really tried to help me. It seemed like a long horror story, but she stuck by me through every bit of it. And during that long recovery period, there began to be big changes in Mom and big changes in me.

Imagine our position. I was with Mom all the time. She had to do things for me—all sorts of things—and it became almost like *she* was *me*. Where I left off, she finished for me. Someone asked if I resented that. No, I never did. I resented Mom a lot of the time before the accident, but never afterwards.

I can look back now and see the position I was in before the accident, and the kind of self-centered person I would have grown up to be. But that all got stopped. Praise God! I can truly thank Him for that accident.

God used my misfortune to bring about a lot of good. He changed me; He changed Mom; He changed our whole family. He made us become so much more considerate and loving. We're much quicker to think of others now. I know He gave me a real compassion for other people.

While I was recovering, Mom was always pushing me to get out a little further, try a little harder, and she helped by encouraging me that I *could* do it. She wasn't critical any more; she was constantly encouraging. For example, she didn't make me walk. She didn't try to *make* me do that or anything else. She'd wait for me and allow me to make my own decisions. She never forced me, just encouraged me, and waited for me to be ready within myself.

My "old" mother didn't have patience like that. My "new" mother had all the patience in the world with me, and so did Dad and Larry Don. They all helped with my re-habilitation.

My dad helped a lot with the physical things. He got me into the swimming pool the second day I was home, and took me in the water every day after that. Larry Don spent hours rubbing Vitamin E oil into my scars, and now they're pretty well invisible. He'd talk to me, teach me the alphabet, tell me jokes. Mom helped me with word transfers; when I'd use the wrong word she'd say, "Stop! What's the word you want there, Kathy?"

Actually, Mom did the most toward reprogramming me, but all my family took part in all kinds of ways. They were so loving and patient. I wouldn't be like I am today—really healed and normal again—if it weren't for them. On the other hand, they wouldn't be like they are today if they hadn't had to do it!

Before my accident, I wouldn't have dreamed of my family acting that way. We were all too busy and self-centered. I provided the means of making all of us slow down. There is *nothing* swift about brain recuperation. My mother had always been the busiest woman you ever saw, but she became determined to teach me to walk, talk, and everything else.

Now that is slow-w-w-w work. It amazed me to see Mom coming up with all that patience.

She had to tutor me full-time that way only for six months, I guess. The accident happened in March, and by September I was ready for school—with the help of tutors and a learning resource center. It was hard. I still was into rehabilitating, which took so much time, and it felt terrible to go to school when you didn't walk or talk right, or even look right, and couldn't relate to your old friends.

I can't describe how discouraged and frustrated I felt. Mom was constantly telling me that with God's help I could do anything and everything, in time. She encouraged and encouraged and encouraged me.

Fortunately, I was a Christian at the time of my accident. And even though I was just a "baby" Christian, I could believe the things Mom was telling me: that God really *cared;* that Jesus would heal me; that my faith was going to help me win. Mom and I really prayed about just *everything,* but then I'd realize I had to put some feet to my faith, and *try.*

My intellect still worked, Mom would remind me, and with God's help I was going to relearn everything, and a few new things besides! She was right. Praise God, I graduated at the right time, and got my grade point average back up to *A*s.

Let me tell you, Mom was the only one who believed those things she kept telling me. I remember early in my freshman year, in that special school I hated so much, when my doctor told me to get adjusted to it. He said I was going to be that way all my life. I didn't like that. In fact, it frustrated me so much, I picked up a paperweight and threw it at him!

It didn't hit him, fortunately, and it didn't make him mad.

In fact he told us that was really good, that I could express my anger.

That day the doctor was just telling the truth as he saw it, and he couldn't say anything real positive about me at that point. But I was so upset that Mom had to get me out of there, and I exploded again in the parking lot. Standing beside our car, I cried and really got upset and told Mom I hated it. I really *hated* that this was the way I'd have to be all the rest of my life.

I'll never forget that day. Mom just took my hand and prayed a little prayer, then started talking to me. She said I *didn't* have to be that way. She reminded me that what I'd heard about me came from a doctor, and he could tell us only technical things. Mom reminded me that with God's help, I'd be able to show him—but the choice was up to me. I could accept that doctor's say-so, or we could keep on working by faith.

I believed Mom. Together we started aiming for the kind of grades I thought I should be making. It was hard, terribly hard. I probably worked four times harder than other kids my age were having to do. My dad would help me with math, Mom with vocabulary. She taught me that anything you write, patterns itself on your brain; so I'd write my vocabulary words and learn them that way. Later I learned them from flash cards, as I exercised on a minitrampoline.

My mother and I were spending hours together every day. I began to share my frustrations, hopes, and all my emotions with her for the first time. She was so understanding and encouraging, always helping me.

That was the first time I knew she could be that kind of an individual. Always before I had seen her as an authority figure, not a person. I believe that's a typical viewpoint young girls have of their mothers, and it's a shame. We love our mothers, but can't share with them in all those ways that mean so much.

By now, I recognized that God gave me a "new" Mom. I also knew that God, through her love and patience, brought a "new" Kathy into being.

I believe I'm more mature than some other girls my age because I've been through a lot more. I know I am my own person, able and willing to decide for myself, with God's help, what's best for me and what I want to do with my life.

For example, I decided not to attend college. This was a hard decision, since many of my friends do go to college, and this would put me out-of-step with my peers. Time has convinced me I made a right decision, because my accident and the events that came out of it have given me some really unusual opportunities.

I believe God wants me to seize those opportunities. I want to go through every door He opens, and my parents feel the same way. My mother and I travel together a great deal. I also spend several hours a day in private Bible study and devotions. I'm involved with the rest of our family in a super business, Amway sales and marketing, which brings all of us into contact with some of the most prominent Christian business leaders in America.

I believe I'm receiving a very special education that is more valid for me right now than anything else I could possibly do. I know it's making me happy, because it's offering me so many ways to grow as a woman.

Of course, I'm spending more time than ever with Mom. We have a really wonderful Christian prayer relationship, and she has become my best friend. I often tell God how much I wish other mothers and daughters could feel this way about each other, and how I know it has to begin with Jesus Christ.

What if my mother had not had Christ to share with me when I was so badly hurt? What if she hadn't known Him (and I mean *really* known Him), could she have urged me every day of my rehabilitation to keep on keeping on with Him? I really doubt it.

I knew the day would come when I'd get a chance to encourage my mother the way she had hung in there with me. Well, recently we flew to California to help get my grandmother adjusted in a nursing home. This was a hard task for Mom, but I was able to encourage her to get down with Grandmother and really love and encourage her as she had done with me. I tried to convince Mom that Grandmother could respond in a positive way.

She was old and sick and took a lot of pills, and sometimes she didn't act too rational. But I remembered how Mom used to reassure me that my intellect still worked, so I believed Grandma's did, too.

That visit changed everything for Mom. It's really neat when a mother and a daughter and a grandmother can all minister to one another the way we did. In fact, I really believe we got a "new" grandma, before she went home to be with the Lord.

Praise the Lord!

Barbara

6
Learning to Love My *Self*

We'd be walking through a shopping mall, my preteen daughter and I, when suddenly I'd poke Kathy with my elbow, give her a sharp nudge and whisper, "Wow! Do you see that fat lady over there?"

That scene occurred rather often, actually. Soon after I accepted Christ into my life and began working with the classes in "Woman—Aware and Choosing," *I* became aware that one of the areas in which I felt much discontent was that of my weight.

Since I was fat, I noticed everyone else who was fat. Now I couldn't be vocal about it, since early in life I'd decided that since my mother was so vocal, I wasn't ever going to be sharp-tongued. So I developed the "art" of the silent nudge, the nod of the head, that said in a nonverbal manner, "Do you see *that,* Kathy?"

Sometimes we'd each giggle or snicker without saying a word, since we both knew what each was thinking about someone we'd spotted. We didn't *need* to say a word. And that's the way *I taught my daughter to be critical.*

I didn't know I was doing that, of course. I know now that I acted that way because I was tremendously unhappy with myself.

Then I went through a time when I lost a tremendous amount of weight, but instead of feeling happy about it, I

got on a kick where I wanted to revolutionize the world. I
wanted to get everybody on a diet and make everybody slim
and trim. Why? I *still* didn't like my Self. And the truth is, I
was afraid of losing ground—afraid I'd become fat again
myself.

It's not easy, necessarily, to learn how to love one's Self.
For one thing, we disguise our dislike (even our self-hatred)
in so many ways. The Bible says in Psalms 139:14 that we
are "fearfully and wonderfully made." I don't know any be-
lievers who haven't come to a point of real dismay, when
they received certain insights as to why they did certain
things.

I'm no exception. Because of all the criticism I displayed,
I'm afraid I caused the early Kathy (seems funny to speak of
"two" Kathys, doesn't it?) to become a very critical little
girl. When I realized what I had done, I can remember going
before God and crying.

"What can I do?" I wept. "I've already set such a bad example!" Through prayer God showed me that by example
we teach our kids both good *and* bad attitudes. I could set
that critical spirit right within my own life, and my daughter
would follow my example.

There's such a danger, in a book like this, of making
everything sound so easy. You see how I did this, then God
did that (which really is true, as far as it goes), and out come
all the pat answers. The fact is, God's principles *are* simple
to grasp, simple to understand—but not necessarily easy to
enact. Even given divine insights such as the instance I just
described, it's still difficult to change our own long-estab-
lished behavior patterns.

The habit of self-dislike seems particularly hard to
change, which is understandable, when we realize that it

began very early in our lives. When we once begin to receive a clear view of our sin of self-hatred and its effects not only in my life but all the others I touch, we can cry out, with the apostle Paul, that "the good that I would I do not: but the evil which I would not, that I do" (Romans 7:19).

What is my answer, then? For me, it came in Romans 8:1, 2 as Paul writes:

> There is therefore now no condemnation to them which are in Christ Jesus, who walk not after the flesh, but after the Spirit. For the law of the Spirit of life in Christ Jesus hath made me free from the law of sin and death.

As I worked with Kathy during her recuperation, I often thought how thankful I was to be given a second chance with her training. I could see so many mistakes I had made with her—mistakes which invariably reflected weakness and sin in my own personality. Is there any worse pain for a parent, than to see his or her own weak traits coming out in his beloved son or daughter?

My own moment of decision came when Kathy first came out of her coma. We had an option to train her in the negative patterns she'd learned the first time, or to begin a whole new way. Some instinct (I know now it was the Holy Spirit of God) directed us to choose the latter course.

There might be animosity among the other members of our family, but never with Kathy. How we treated her meant the difference between life and death, and we were determined not to feed her any garbage. I concentrated on creating harmony for her. (*Why is it so hard to understand that it is life or death for us all?*)

Five years earlier, when I first accepted Christ, I found

myself so out of line as a Christian. Without realizing it, I had gotten out of fellowship with my husband, and had begun trying to take over as head of our home. There was a quiet, unspoken sort of power struggle between Larry and me, one so subtle that we—not knowing the will of God about marriage—could not identify.

I had wandered way out of the zone of love because of my frustrations, and I was trying to find out who I was. Actually, I suppose that identity crisis had begun ten years before the accident. I'd ask myself, *Who am I? I have all these labels, but who am I, really?* I was about age twenty-seven at the time, and it was my first opportunity to get around to such questions.

Larry and I had become engaged and married when I was nineteen, Larry Don was born ten months later. Three years beyond that, Kathy was born. We traveled, Larry had a demanding career as a professional baseball player, and I lost myself in the children.

Larry worked superhard to qualify as a major league player, and made it. What I did, meanwhile, was give my own identity away to become Mrs. Larry Miller. I suppose that's the mistake so many young women make. I was so in awe and enamored of Larry Miller—saw all those great qualities—and didn't believe for one minute that he ever could fall short of perfection.

Take the area of decision making. I gave up my right to make decisions, or even to give Larry input so he could make them. I thought he was so wonderful—that he always chose the right thing—so I allowed him to make all choices.

Larry decided where to go to dinner, how we'd entertain, what movie we'd see, or what color to paint our apartment.

That sounds pretty dumb, but the truth is, it's easy to get so engrossed in someone else you forget *you* also have an identity.

Later, as the children grew, I'd gotten so used to passing responsibilities over to Larry that I'd automatically tell them, when they misbehaved: "Wait till your father comes home. You're going to get in trouble!"

That's not right, of course. It wasn't fair to Larry or to me. Gradually, as I allowed myself to hide behind Larry, I erased my own personality. The bubbly, vivacious woman who first attracted Larry simply ceased to exist. She was hiding behind a listless, frumpy person who had allowed herself to get fat.

How did I erase myself? Step by step, through cookies, big sandwiches, a wonderful piece of cake, or a big dish of ice cream. No wonder I could not like myself. How could I love the "nothing" I'd allowed myself to become? Where was the starting place?

For me, Matthew 7:7, 8 held the key. Jesus said:

"Ask, and it shall be given you; seek, and ye shall find; knock, and it shall be opened unto you: For every one that asketh receiveth; and he that seeketh findeth; and to him that knocketh it shall be opened."

My "asking, seeking, and knocking" took many forms. God leads us from one piece of useful insight or knowledge to the next, when we truly seek Him. As the apostle Paul said, ". . . he which hath begun a good work in you will perform it until the day of Jesus Christ" (Philippians 1:6).

From Christian books, seminars, church services, prayer groups, teachers, and my own prayers and observations,

God gradually helped Barbara Miller begin to like herself and love herself and accept herself *as she is, unconditionally, no strings attached.*

I admit I had to do a lot of seeking concerning this problem. Doubtless, also, my greatest advances came through the area of professional counseling—counseling undertaken not in behalf of me, but for our son, who came to suffer grave problems with drugs and alcohol, following Kathy's tragic accident.

Had I known, when I first asked, "God, who am I?" that the question eventually must be answered through the intense sufferings of Larry Don, I could not have borne it. However, just as the reprogramming begun in Kathy resulted in great inner healing for her mother, so did Larry Don's counseling result in still further healing for me, for my husband, and for our family as a unit.

How can I learn to love myself? Jesus said, "Seek, and ye shall find."

Is it worth the effort and the pain? Perhaps you've come to that same question in your life: *Who am I?*

Or perhaps you've come to that later question: *Lord, how can I love my Self?*

The only answer—the only answer at all—lies in the name of Jesus Christ. As He said in John 15:4:

> "Abide in me, and I in you. As the branch cannot bear fruit of itself, except it abide in the vine; no more can ye, except ye abide in me."

I could not learn to love my Self until I first loved Him. As He said in the next verse, "Without me ye can do nothing."

Amen.

Three generations: Barbara's mom, Doris Barlow, with her mother, Gertrude Jennings, and Barbara. *Below:* Three more generations: Kathy, her grandmother, Doris Barlow, and her mother, Barbara.

Kathy writes in one of her *feelin'* books as her dog, Pepper, keeps her company.

Barbara and Kathy on a speaking tour. After her severe injuries and long coma, who would have expected Kathy to speak to audiences all over the country! There were eighteen thousand attending the Dexter Yeager Family Reunion in North Carolina, where this picture was taken. *Right:* On Thanksgiving Day 1977, Kathy performed basic eye exercises (part of her recovery program set up by Barbara) for her appreciative grandmother.

A snapshot of the young family during Larry's baseball career: baby Kathy, Barbara, Larry Don. *Below:* Here's the family today: Kathy, Dad, Mom, Larry Don.

Kathy and Barbara were close, even before the accident. During her long recuperative period, however, Kathy realized she had a "new" mom and she was a "new" Kathy. This was taken when Kathy was named Homecoming Queen. *Below:* Kathy with her mother and grandmother. Writes Kathy, "It's really neat when a mother and a daughter and a grandmother can all minister to one another the way we did."

Barbara discusses the importance of communication. She and Kathy have lots of opportunities to share, as they travel around the country on personal-appearance tours. Here they pose next to John Davidson's Rolls-Royce after an NBC taping. *Right:* The Millers also share their ideas on communication during their speaking appearances, such as this one for the Women's Ministry.

Barbara was named "Arizona Mother of the Year" in 1979. Few realized then how hard Barbara and Larry had had to work to save their marriage and family relationships. *Below:* The Millers at the award banquet, looking like the Ideal American Family.

7

Gettin' Down and Doin' It

Hi, again! I'm glad to write chapter 7, since seven is God's symbol of perfection; and I really like my topic: *gettin' down and doin' it.* That's the secret to almost anything, in my opinion: making up your mind to change, to get going. Someday I want to write a whole book on how to do that.

As Mom and I travel and meet so many people, I often get acquainted with other girls who tell me their problems. There's always trouble at home. They don't like, or love, or respect their mothers. They tell me I'm lucky to have the kind of mother I have, and they're right—but that's not the whole answer. The other part is, what kind of daughter does the *mother* have?

So many times we girls have a stubborn attitude. It's all the mother's fault—nothing's wrong with *us.* Yes, you're right. I used to be that way, too! In that frame of mind, we're not hearing the Lord's call on our lives. We're wanting to put the blame for everything on someone else. We won't take responsibility, and aren't ready to face the truth: that if *we're* not ready to get down and do it, nothing will get any better. There's plenty of responsibility to being a daughter, you know.

In a bad mother-daughter situation, somebody needs to be willing to bend a little. I think it should be the mother, since she's older and has had more experience. But from another standpoint, I think the daughter should do it, out of respect for her mother.

My mother and I both learned to yield to one another because it's right to do this: we want, more than anything else, to please the Lord; and we want to love one another. It takes a real willingness to bend.

When I was younger, I had friends whose mothers didn't show them any respect, who called them names, even cursed them, and showed all sorts of contempt every way you can imagine. Those girls would say, "I can't love her. I don't want to love my mother."

Sometimes the mothers actually appeared *jealous* of their daughters. Maybe the girls had nicer things, a better house and clothes—whatever—than the mother did, growing up; or maybe these mothers didn't have the room or the space to share the fathers with their daughters. Situations like that can get really bad on everybody.

Still, it's nothing the Lord can't heal. I meet hundreds of girls who claim they can't love their mothers, but that's not true. In the Ten Commandments, God tell us to love our parents. If God tells us to do something, we can do it. If we don't love our parents it's because we *decided* not to love them.

The good side of the subject is, I've seen many girls change dramatically towards their parents—especially after the young women came to know the Lord Jesus Christ. I know I changed! On the other hand, many refuse to let go of that anger and rebellion. They think they can get along okay without loving their fathers or mothers, but personally I believe they're missing out on something terrifically important.

If they don't learn how to get along at home today, how will they handle getting along in marriage tomorrow?

So suppose you're enduring a really bad situation at home with your parents. Where is the starting place? What's all this about *gettin' down and doin' it?*

I'd say, first of all, decide there'll be some changes made. The place for me to start is with *myself,* starting from the inside and working out. The most important thing is, I've got to work on my mind, my attitude, my train of thought. Then everything else can fall into place.

You say, *"How,* Kathy?" For me, it's with a pen and a notebook. I begin to write down my hopes and dreams, what I want in my life, and then I take a real good look at what I've written. Next, I just give those things to the Lord.

When we give our mind to God, then get into the Bible and become willing to listen to Him direct our lives, through the working of His Spirit, that's where real life begins. *That's* gettin' down and doin' it.

Suppose a girl really hates herself, hates her parents, hates school, and everything else about her life. She's really messed up. She's convinced *nobody* could straighten all that out.

Do you know Somebody can? Just make a list of everything terrible that's bothering you, then get down and turn the whole list over to Jesus. That's the starting place. Let Him take over: tell Him all your feelings. Let go and let God, and you'll get that tremendous peace inside, and you'll be able to get up and go to work on changing *you.*

Then what? After starting with the girl inside, how about you on the outside? Do you like what you see? Usually when we get ourselves really messed up, we even hate the way we look. It's interesting how many girls who're depressed, who consider themselves failures, who suffer with bad mother-daughter problems, also have a *weight* problem. Overweight seems to be a real symptom of unhappiness.

Many times when we're overweight, we're rebellious, and we eat whatever we want whenever we want it, and don't care about the outcome. That's a self-discipline problem, and it *shows*. Also, our self-esteem and confidence is low, so we eat to compensate.

Well, for the girl who hasn't got hold of any kind of self-discipline, it makes sense to start improving her own body. After all, my body is where I live. After I get that looking good, I can begin to feel good about myself—which gives me the space to love myself, and then begin to love others.

Yes, loving my Self will require discipline on my part. So, I'd suggest getting to work on your appearance. Work on your weight. And when your mom sees that you mean business about your own appearance, she will respect you for that and things will begin to improve between you.

Then, there's the subject of a girl's room. It should be kept clean and neat. Most every girl I've ever heard of has had parent problems because of her room, and sometimes I was no exception. My dad was really strict. In a way, I didn't need his strictness about that. I inherited his desire to see things always looking just so, and I learned more from his example than from his words. I wanted to copy his habits.

But if a girl lives like a slob, she can change her whole life by making the simple decision to clean up her room and make it work better for her. It's easier to live in and operate from if you've got it the way you want it.

Straighten out your appearance, your room, your space— and those habits will start carrying over into all the things parents get on our backs about. Homework. Telephone habits. Politeness. Making it to places on time.

Speaking of time, how do you spend yours? These days I

don't have unlimited time to visit other girls and just lounge around. There's too much to do, and you have to allot certain amounts of time for certain things. This book, for example. Mom and I have really done some talking, thinking and praying about this project!

Then there's Bible study, which I like to do early each day. There's my wardrobe to take care of, little notes to write, exercise, housekeeping—and packing. We're always packing or unpacking.

Some girls never find time to get around to some of those simple things I mentioned, because they haven't scheduled them into their lives. I've learned that if you're not disciplined, you can't go with the flow. I have to keep my things in order, my life up-to-date, or it's not going to be possible for me to travel and do all the other neat things that pop up. I really believe that when a girl decides to shape up, the Lord sends opportunities to her that she never dreamed of!

Another thing, kids can give time to their parents. If you really want to help the mother-daughter relationship, you're going to have to be willing to give of yourself. You'll need to learn to listen to your mother, too. (I mean, *really* listen.)

Some mothers, like mine, tend to overextend themselves. They overload themselves with obligations, then they get hassled and depressed and even cranky. They start snapping or yelling at everybody. That suits some kids just fine. They say, well, that's *her* problem. Really, it's everybody's problem, and a God-given opportunity for me to help my mom in a meaningful way at a time when she really appreciates it.

I really want to do everything I can to help her. I do it in little ways, mostly in the office and around the house. I help her with tapes, filing, small business tasks—that kind of thing. I also dust, do dishes, cook a meal, or whatever else I see needs doing. Mom never asks me; I just sense the need and follow through. I enjoy it. It gives her pleasure.

Another way I've learned to help, is that she and I talk and share about what's going on. She likes to get my input. Also, I tell her about my various boyfriends and ask her opinions and advice, and I listen. I really listen. When I think her advice is wise, I'm glad to apply it. Actually, I take a lot of advice from Mom and I'm glad to get it.

I didn't use to think that my mother and I were very much alike, but now I see we have many temperament traits in common. However, in a couple of ways I'm a lot like Dad. For example, I'm really easygoing. I don't let things affect me.

It amazes and amuses Mom that I have this ability to know when I simply need to stop everything and rest. A fif-teen-minute catnap really recharges my batteries, so I fall asleep in the car, or the kitchen, the sofa, or wherever. I think it keeps me on an even keel.

Somebody asked, "Is that because of your injury?" No, I've *always* done this. Even in first grade I'd come home from school and take a rest, before I expected myself to begin accomplishing things. You do better homework that way.

I consider rest an important part of self-discipline. I like to go out in the evenings to movies, concerts, or dinner just as much as the next guy, but unless you've got good rest habits, those late hours sure show up in your face and dis-position.

If you train yourself to keep a steady pace, that is really the best possible discipline, I believe. Dad says I always paced myself. Even in first grade, I'd know to do my homework without anybody making me do it. I guess that's a little unusual, but I'd figured out that if I'd just do my work on some kind of steady schedule, I never had to catch up. I was always finished while some other kids were behind.

Even before first grade, they expected me to make my bed and tidy my room. My dad was really strict about order and neatness, but I never minded that he was strict. I always respected and admired my father and wanted to be like him in regards to self-discipline—and I am. Anyhow, he's not a heavy father. He's a really loving, hugging, touching kind of guy. He's also very handsome, and I enjoy having a nice-looking father.

When you have really good-looking parents, like Larry Don and I do, it's neat when kids appreciate them for that. Most kids would like that privilege, but their mothers and fathers aren't that well-disciplined themselves. They let their own looks go, then give all those good excuses about it. I believe kids want their parents to set a better example than that!

When the parents don't have enough self-esteem to take proper care of themselves, their weight, their looks and so on, naturally their children can grow up with the same kind of low self-worth. I believe good-looking parents are happier people, and have more fun loving and kidding around with their kids.

So we're back to what Mom said about relationships— that low self-esteem is at the bottom of any bad setup like that. Whether it's the mother, the daughter, even the grandmother, each woman needs to get right with the Lord, then get right with her Self.

If you want to change your feelings toward your Self into a whole new life-style, just try these few simple suggestions for even just thirty days. If they don't work, let me know. If they do, praise God!

Here's that list:

GETTIN' DOWN AND *DOIN'* IT

1. Turn your dreams and your problems over to God. Ask Jesus to come into your life and change you.

2. Decide what you want to change about yourself. Start with one thing (if you're overweight, why not start with that!) and make definite plans to change.

3. Take a good look at your room, and ask yourself if you're happy with your present surroundings, or ready to improve them.

4. Keep a journal for thirty days. Each day write down your successes. Make a note of everything that changes for the better, and praise God for His help. Where you fail, just start over. Don't hate yourself. Forgive yourself as God forgives you.

5. Be honest when you look at some of the things your parents or teachers don't like about you. If you have a sassy mouth, if you're lazy or late, or never do your homework, at least don't lie to *yourself* about it. Just take one thing at a time. You can't change it all overnight.

6. When people compliment you on the changes they see, thank them graciously. Give God the credit.

7. When your girl friends notice a different you, share what is happening. Maybe they'd like to try some new ways too!

Now take another look at those seven suggestions. Do you agree that they could give you a whole new life? Help your parents respect you? Give you back the self-esteem you lost, back there somewhere?

One thing for sure, it's your choice. Take the first tiny step, though, and the Lord will help you with the rest of it. You'll find that anger and rebellion slipping right off your shoulders, like a hot, scratchy sweater you no longer need.

You're gonna *love* the new you!

8
Opening Up

People joke with me that I'm just a born talker. The truth is, talking is not communicating. Discovering true communication became a tremendous revelation to me. It has changed my life!

How can we learn to communicate? In my case, I learned the hard way. At first, as you remember, there were no words from Kathy. Mute and helpless, totally dependent, she couldn't transmit her thoughts at all via words. So I learned early that I must listen for any sound at all, and I became very good at reading her "body language."

For example, as I'd notice Kathy's smooth brow, marred only by the slash of a scar above one eyebrow, I'd see the eyebrows lift in an interesting way, as she formed thoughts. If she struggled with a problem, I'd see her little brow wrinkle.

Long before the sparkle returned to Kathy's eyes, I became aware of those brooding, expressionless blue pools as they "trailed" me, following my path as I moved about the room. Sometimes I'd see a tiny tear form in the corner of her eye, but never did it roll down her cheek. She did not have the ability to cry.

If she disliked something, or felt anger rising, she'd wrinkle her nose in a little snit. Her nostrils would flare, and she'd draw her nose up, ever so tight. At other times, when she didn't want to cooperate, she'd turn her cheek—as if to block me out. Those were tough times, yet quite normal during rehabilitation. I'd touch that little cheek with my hand and say, "It's okay, babe. It's going to be all right."

This process made me keenly aware of how much all of us communicate beyond what our mouths actually speak. It also made me conscious that I'd done a lot of talking to my children—and very little listening. (They could have told me that, of course, but I wouldn't have been listening if they had!)

With Kathy, I learned quickly that in order to "hear" her I must learn to be totally open. I must learn not to function as a stone wall, hard and unyielding and resistant, but must become a parachute. It meant total retraining for me. It meant open mind versus closed mind. I found it tremendously difficult and challenging. Like Kathy, I was relearning some important brain patterns!

As her brain made its comeback, Kathy experienced a period when she'd see or hear something which would trigger a memory. It was a very interesting process—sort of a flashback—but the part of her thinking that ordinarily would have inhibited her from saying certain things had not yet returned. Consequently she'd say anything, anytime, to anyone, and she'd spare no detail. When one of those flashbacks occurred, she really told it like it was.

One day she and I drove past a house where Kathy once had attended a party. She said, "We're at a party, Mom. Wow! Such strange things are happening at the party."

"Tell me about it," I encouraged.

"Boy, the place is really a mess. I'm busy cleaning up, because the parents will be upset when they get home. I want their house to look nice."

I said, "Kathy, was the place a mess when you arrived, or did you kids make it a mess?"

"Well, the kids made it a mess," she related. "The parents are not at home: they went to another party. Mom, you should see [and she called the girl's name]. Boy, is she acting dumb. She's running through the house with nothing on but her bra and panties."

"Kathy, look again," I suggested. "Maybe she's wearing a swimsuit."

"No," she replied steadily. "She has her bra and panties on and is acting like she's drunk. You should see her, Mom. They threw her in the shower, and she's acting so stupid, but you should see how she shapes up when the police come!

"She's not really drunk, Mom. . . ."

Had Kathy's accident not occurred, she'd never have told me that story, of course. But the recollections would come so swiftly, so vividly, and through hearing them I knew I wanted and needed to become my daughter's confidante. I decided that no matter what she told me, I must not act shocked, or turn off her opportunity to confide.

Nor could I act judgmental or condemning, no matter what came out. So I'd brace myself for such stories, knowing that something in her brain was temporarily malfunctioning, that she was about to disclose things she'd otherwise never tell.

We knew about that party, Larry and I. We knew the police had come, that her dad came to get her, that she was grounded—but I knew nothing about the inside story. Actually, I never asked her, at the time; or maybe I did, but then didn't listen.

Now, however, during that particular flashback, I asked Kathy, "Do you see yourself drinking?"

"No, Mom," came the instant reply. "That's why I was cleaning house, so I wouldn't have to get involved. Then I went out to the horse corral so I could stay uninvolved."

I winced, remembering. It had been one of those deals where each girl told her mother that the other mothers said it was okay, so, being busy, we didn't check it out. Here were these little eighth-grade kids drinking beer and wine and necking on couches and in the corners, acting rowdy, and the police came.

Now I thought, *She didn't feel free to call home and say, "Come get me. I'm someplace I don't belong."*

Had Kathy told me about that party before her accident, I would have been horrified. What would people think about my daughter at a party where all this stuff was going on? She was only in the eighth grade!

At a certain age, I think, even a child who normally does communicate with her parents pretty well might begin to adopt the "what they don't know won't hurt them" attitude. I'm sure that happens when a mother acts critical about so many things that the child knows not to bring forward *any* news that explosive.

So Kathy didn't describe the party. She knew the "old" Barbara would listen in horror, then scream, "You're absolutely grounded!" How quick we are to ground kids. An eighth-grader can get into a situation that's beyond her depth and not know how to get herself out of it. She needs the freedom to discuss these messes openly, figure them out, then learn how to handle similar situations in the future.

Today, the inhibitory area of Kathy's brain functions perfectly, but she still confides in me. We have an open relationship. Mothers always envision that kind of openness and closeness with their daughters, but before her accident, Kathy and I never had it.

When we allow our kids to really tell it all, and we're not so quick to judge or condemn, but simply there to listen, they'll make themselves available for guidance. Suppose your child runs in to tell you something that happened: "Gosh, Mom, guess what happened today?"

As his eyes dart back and forth, watching your eyes to read your expression, he gauges exactly how much of the story he can tell. If I'm a "wall," I'll get very few details of that story. But if I'm a "parachute," open to really hearing ... "Gosh, tell me what happened! Show me what you did today! How did it go at the party? Tell me what you saw! What was it really like?" With those responses, watch those eyes as they look into yours; just listen as the story starts coming forth!

Before, I was some sort of Dismay Machine. I felt it my duty to register shock, horror, whatever seemed appropriate, if my kids told me something of which I did not approve. Little by little, I was closing our doors of communication.

When I did learn to listen, however, I learned we can say: "Let's look at that from a different perspective. Have you ever thought ... ?" "I want to propose a new angle. Have you considered that ... ?"

We're able to offer alternatives. Also, we usually don't have to tell a teenager what's right or wrong; they nearly always can tell us. It's more that we act as a guide. We encourage and enable our children to arrive at their own wise choices. Not only does this show them we expect them to choose prudently, but also that we have confidence that they will do it.

As I became willing to listen, Kathy became more willing

to confide. In turn, as we learned how to open up to one another, I learned to confide in my daughter.

I'd return from a shopping trip, for example, and dash into the house and go from room to room seeking Kathy, eager to share something I'd just thought or seen. I'd curl up beside her on the couch, eager to chat, full of news, unable to wait to fill her in.

On the other hand, I might tell her, "Something is really bugging me. Just let me talk it through, and then let's pray about it."

That was a brand-new area of experience for me. I knew how to talk, okay, but never had I trained myself to express my true feelings in a precise way—not blown out of perspective, not exaggerated, not forced. It's very important to learn to listen without judging. It's equally important to learn how to share feelings with another person, to receive hers and deliver yours.

Kathy taught me a lot about that sort of transaction. She's very good at doing this, because she's a good journalist. She calls her journals her *feelin'* books, and they truly are a record of her honest reactions to life as she finds it. She's a private person. She doesn't share her written feelings, ordinarily, so I was pleased that she opened up some of those precious books to reveal some bits for this book.

None of this could have happened in the old days, when I'd have been forming a reply, even as my children tried to confide in me. I was like a wall in those days—a wall that shut them out. Larry Don and Kathy knew it, too!

Because I was so guilty of that, today I love being a parachute. You see, that openness gives me just as much freedom and nonjudgment as it does the other person! By contrast, I meet many other parents who fear the judgment of their own child, even though that parent, like me, had taught the child judging, by example.

Today I want *anything* that comes from Larry Don's or Kathy's mouth to come out freely, with no condemnation from me. Proverbs 31:26, part of the famous passage which describes the godly woman, says, "She openeth her mouth with wisdom." I've learned I can do so much good with my mouth. I've also learned that it's very easy to use my lips as a deadly instrument, ready to hurt and tear down others. It's my choice.

That brings me to the subject of verbal attacks, which have caused me and so many others untold pain in our lives. As soon as Kathy and I embarked on this book, it seemed that a rash of such attacks broke out here and there. My first reaction said, "Lord, who do I think I am, trying to write this book? My own home is so imperfect. There's so much in each of us to work on."

So Kathy and I decided that when we got into a snit, or had words, we'd simply analyze what happened, try to make it useful. We aren't trying to present ourselves as perfect, anyhow! And that's just what we did.

One day Kathy and I were someplace when a problem arose, so she and I went to the back of the room and tried to put our new skills to work. We tried to discover the reason for an attack, rather than attacking the attacker. We decided it boiled down once again to that basic problem with self-esteem.

Who am I? *That old question again.* True, I'm Kathy Miller's mother, I reminded her, but that's not the only person I am. I am many persons, actually.

Then we tackled the idea of communication. We decided it was important for me to share my feelings, and she needed to listen without judging. When we got to the next step, I simply wrote, "Let go and let God." We saw that so many times when things get tense, we try to manipulate or control the circumstances or the other person.

We can change some problems, but there are some we can't change. In that case it's truly beautiful to give that problem to God and let Him take care of it.

Finally, there's tremendous power in "binding the adversary." (We realized that particular attack was satanic.) There *is* a devil, and he constantly bombards the world with darkness. When we realize that, we don't have to respond personally. By the authority given us by Jesus Christ, we can follow His instructions to His disciples in Matthew 18:18, bind our adversary, and refuse to entertain him and his tricks.

Remember, I told Kathy, that Satan piles fear, doubt, discouragement, and condemnation on us—or tries to. Interestingly enough, however, we can train our minds in exactly the opposite direction. We can visualize strength, joy, power, victory, love—all Christ's characteristics—alive in us.

Many of us inherited the tendency to expect the bad, the wrong, the failure, to happen. This strain runs through some families, from generation to generation, like brown eyes or curly hair. But if just one person would break that attitude cycle—would reprogram his mind to think on the positive side—to foresee possibilities—to see with the eyes of faith. . . .

If I train myself to look for what can go *right* instead of what can go *wrong*, my children probably will pass that trait along to their kids. I'm saying, "Let's give living space to God, not Satan!"

People say, "Yes, but that doesn't come naturally." The truth is, it *does* come naturally. When mothers and dads attempt to think as God thinks, on what is pure, just, true, and beautiful, the children naturally will catch that attitude from the parents. The home atmosphere begins to clear up, and peace dwells there.

Opening up. It's not easy, learning to be vulnerable and transparent before your husband and children, much less all the others to whom we relate. Communication must be worked at; acceptance must be learned; forgiveness must be utilized.

With all that, however, God has given us a marvelous special gift—the gift of touching. With any crisis of communication, there's such a tremendous need simply to touch and be touched. No wonder the Scripture tells us about the laying on of hands!

Think what a hunger we have for touching: the soft touch of a hand; a firm hug; an arm around the shoulder. Every person needs all of this, and more. In fact, psychologists tell us the average human being needs some fourteen touches a day, in order to stay emotionally well nourished.

Think of that! How many times have you been touched today? Your husband? Your children? Your mother?

For Barbara Miller, touching was the easy part. Not so easy, however, were some of the other ways God wanted to teach me to open up. *Listening. Expressing feelings. Dealing with verbal attacks. Allowing God into my situation. Dealing with the devil. Feeding my mind a good diet of godly thoughts.*

Thanks to Kathy, I learned to become a parachute. I'm learning how to open up, to float, to travel softly. Of course, I knew I needed to change, especially since it would so obviously affect my daughter's future. Ironically, however, I didn't realize my son was walking on the razor's edge—that his life teetered in the balance fully as much as did his sister's.

And above all, I certainly didn't know that unless I could change, Larry Miller and I were traveling a collision course. Our marriage was speeding toward failure.

9
The Way We Were

We'd settled into a so-called typical marriage, meaning not too good, not too bad. Actually nobody seemed all that unhappy, but still, as a good Christian wife will do, I decided we should be happier and began reading some of the "good wife" books.

Now I knew, as a "good wife," to take particular pains to see that Larry always got the hearty breakfast he so enjoyed. I had begun to play that game called How-do-I-get-what-I-want-by-giving-you-what-you-need?

Larry's clock runs opposite to mine; he is not a morning person. But I'm an early riser, a naturally happy, peppy person in the A.M., so it was easy for me to zoom into the kitchen and get his breakfast going, even as I instructed the kids and placed a couple of early business phone calls.

Larry's eggs would be waiting, and he'd still be in the bathroom getting ready for work. I'd dial another phone number. When Larry did reach the kitchen, he'd see me with my ear to the phone—so he'd just wave and head on out, and when I got off the phone I'd be *furious!* There I'd be, staring at "the usual," two eggs over easy, bacon on the side, and toast.

Then I'd really have to work to get over my anger. Some mornings it took an hour or two of praying, singing, doing

whatever I could to chase the fury from my thoughts. It sure
didn't help a lot, either, the time or two when I dressed and
went downtown to a coffee shop we both liked, only to hear
one of the cute waitresses say, "Oh, Mrs. Miller, you have
the *nicest* husband."

"Tell me about it," I'd say. (By then I really *needed* to
know he was nice.)

"He's so thoughtful! He was here for breakfast this
morning. . . ."

"What did he eat for breakfast?" I broke in. (I had to ask.
After all, I'm only human.)

"Oh, you know, 'the usual.' Two eggs over easy, bacon on
the side, toast. . . ."

By now I'd really be fuming. I'd say to myself, *The same
doggoned thing he walked away from at home!*

I couldn't understand about Larry. Everybody was always
saying he was so wonderful. *He's handsome, cheerful, nice,
considerate, all those good things,* I thought—*but that's when
he's away from home. At home, he's* terrible!

That's a quick glimpse of Larry and Barbara Miller—the
way we were. Operating on two separate tracks, failing to
communicate, each wanting to be Number One.

Willliam James, America's pioneer psychologist, said,
"The deepest principle in human nature is the craving to be
appreciated." In those days, not only did Larry and I not
feel loved, but neither of us felt appreciated. We simply
walked (or more likely hustled) through one meaningless
day after another, wondering why life seemed so stupid and
flat, and seeking some sort of self-fulfillment which could fill
the void.

My identity search took me straight to Jesus Christ, so I

asked my questions of Him. *Who am I? Where am I going? What shall I do with my life?*

Larry's identity search, of course, began when he left baseball—and it was painful. After devoting nine years to professional baseball, pitching for the Los Angeles Dodgers and the New York Mets during his final seasons, no wonder he suffered re-entry problems, as he once again began to deal with the ordinary world.

Like so many men, Larry could not verbalize his feelings. Indeed, if I wanted to talk about them, he'd walk out of the room. Meantime, he enrolled in classes at Arizona State University, finished a master's degree in civil engineering, and entered an entirely new job field. Today we know Larry didn't want to be an engineer, but ended in that slot because aptitude tests showed he had a natural proficiency and excellence in the natural sciences.

Larry studied hard all those years and he did very well as an engineer, both professionally and financially. However he wasn't happy. All that time I saw him as floundering.

If Larry intended to flounder, I thought, Barbara had better take over. Old patterns of being the fixer-upper surfaced. He fretted continually about our finances, so I decided to go into business for myself.

I knew whatever business I chose would have to require a low initial investment and be run from my own home. After looking around at numerous opportunities I chose to develop an Amway business. I had used the products and found them to be excellent. Furthermore, I discovered that the Amway marketing concept allowed me the option of teaching others to distribute the products and, in time, develop a substantial business. Since I had always been people oriented and liked to teach others, the Amway business became a natural outlet for my energies.

I decided to take over and be the leader, the decision maker, and the head of the house.

Right there we got even further off the track. God intends the man to lead and the woman to submit to the man, but I was anything but submissive. *If Larry wants to find out who he is, then I'll give him the space to do it,* I reasoned. *Meantime, I'm going to keep this family together.* So I got very, *very* busy. When my children tried to talk to me in the evenings, I usually had my head in the dishwasher. I was planning where I'd go that evening, thinking *I'm going to get this business going—really built up*—all that stuff.

Strangely enough, Larry was forever talking about finances; yet the busier I became and the more money we had, the more he spent. I stayed on a merry-go-round, trying to catch up, earn more, do more, and be more. Things got worse.

I stayed so strung out, playing Wonder Woman. Worst of all, it seemed that no matter how hard I worked, Larry never gave me praise, but only noticed what was *not* done. His criticism usually took a nonverbal form: slamming a door, conspicuously picking things up, looking for a clean shirt.

I was quick to take that sort of thing personally. I seemed to stay on the lookout for criticism, and our life-style offered plenty of chances for receiving it. By the time Larry had phased into engineering, and we found ourselves with two careers going, our home life had become pretty unrewarding.

Certainly there's nothing wrong with enjoying a two-career family—if the family structure has been well established in the first place. If the family is rightly related, you have freedom to take on all sorts of things.

Larry and I, however, did not have common goals. Further, we were far from being submitted to God's idea of how a family should be: God first, husband next, then the wife, and finally the children. Everything in our home seemed out of joint, and my answer was to work harder, to the point where I—like my mother before me—became a workaholic.

I experienced three major surgeries within three years. As a new Christian, I'd find myself lying in bed, saying, "God, I don't understand this. Why am I here?" I had become very abusive to my body, what with overwork, stress, and the continual tensions in our home. There was Barbara, making so many of the decisions—barking the orders—telling people what needed to be done—and all the time, returning to the pattern I had known from my childhood home.

It was a very uncomfortable, yet *familiar* pattern. You can enter a "comfort zone" that's actually *uncomfortable,* but you stay there because it's familiar.

So that's the way we were—something of a portrait of our family—at the time of Kathy's accident. From one point of view, we appear absolutely fragmented, each going in his own direction; but from God's point of view, something exciting was happening. Without our realizing it, our way of escape was in the works!

My Amway sales and marketing business, the first I'd ever operated, proved successful. I discovered I was competent, and the feeling of success almost overwhelmed me, since I didn't know I *could* be successful. I learned I was good at motivating people, and since Larry and I had so little communication between us, meeting and relating to other people filled some of those deep needs for me.

It was at a business meeting one evening that a man remarked, "My sister has written a book I believe you'd enjoy. A lot of the principles she sets forth in her book I hear coming forward from you. I'd like your opinion of what she has written."

When I read the book *Woman: Aware and Choosing,* I got so excited. So many of the answers I'd sought seemed wrapped up in that one good package. Immediately I set out to bring Betty Coble, the author, to Scottsdale for a seminar. The next four years found me teaching Betty Coble's material.

Those classes proved to be the Holy Spirit's training ground where I was concerned. As I began to learn how God intended His principles to operate in practical everyday life, He answered so many of the questions that had sent me running to books, to people, to classes and seminars—all that seeking we do.

You see, as I built my Amway business and worked with more and more people, I noticed something fascinating. Almost invariably, I saw that people will rise to a certain place, then find it impossible to move to the next level. I knew that was true in my life, and I saw many others like me, so I thought, *How can I get a handle on helping people to become more than they are?*

How could we not just *aspire* to be more, but *actually* become more? The thing that hindered, it seemed to me after long involvement with Betty Coble's course, was that old problem of low self-esteem. Again and again I saw it. I saw it in my own home, not just with me, but with each of the ones I loved.

When Kathy's accident hit us all, I had been teaching Betty Coble's course for four years and had begun truly to absorb many of its principles. It proved to be the "how-to" God used not just to help reprogram Kathy, but also her mother—and then her brother—and her father—and our marriage, our home, just began to come together again.

Before all that could happen, however, the situation between Larry and me grew much, much worse. In an academic sense, I knew what God expects a wife to be. Behaviorwise I still was failing, because I had taken so many of Larry's responsibilities upon myself. I took over the disciplining of the children, for example. I protected Larry Don from his father, because I felt if his father stepped in, it would result in a fight. Thus I took away from Larry the responsibility to deal with his own son. That was wrong of me.

Also I thought he shouldn't worry about even the least thing around the house. If something broke, I didn't tell him. And when we became so financially pressed that they threatened to cut off our water or telephone, I shielded Larry from knowing about it. I wanted to protect him from all that pressure and worry, and (of course) I thought I was doing the right thing!

Instead, I was calling all the shots, never asking his advice on business decisions, and meanwhile robbing him of his right to be head of our house, and of the opportunity to grow into those responsibilities. I only wanted to "do my share," but the results were not good. I had begun to emasculate my husband.

Externally, our lives were terribly out of kilter. Internally, an exciting series of changes already had begun to take place within my thinking and desires. God used Kathy's horrible accident as a catalyst—not just for me, but for each of us. With that one stroke, He redeemed our entire family.

Let me pause here and tell about the little gold key I wear on a chain around my neck. It helps me remember that I must reinforce my "positives," and let Jesus handle my "negatives." Every time I taught, I urged the girls to get themselves a key, as a reminder of two things:

> 1. I am responsible for my behavior, but not responsible for any other person's behavior. If I'm happy, sad, glad, mad (or any of those things), that's my own choice.
> 2. There is absolutely nothing that can happen to me today that's too big for God and me to handle.

The instant our neighbor ran in to tell us about Kathy's accident, those principles clicked into place. I immediately went to our key board for my car keys—and the instant I saw those keys, paused for prayer, and *remembered* to be affirmative as I prayed: *Thank You, Lord, for showing me how I need to respond to this situation.*

Larry always says it impressed him that as we drove toward the accident site, I prayed aloud, and especially that I prayed for God to help the man whose car had hit our daughter. I do not remember any of that. Truly God's Spirit had taken me over, was guiding me and praying through me, during those moments and long afterward.

From the moment I touched those car keys, God gave me a supernatural peace and guidance that carried me through the ten and one-half long weeks Kathy lay in a coma. Larry suffered terribly during that time. I know now that, except for that indescribable peace of God I felt, Larry's suffering would have been enough in itself to tear me up, quite apart from the heartbreaking state of our daughter.

God had given me the tools to handle this situation. I knew what I had to do. I understood I had to submit Kathy to God. I had to relinquish her totally. I had to come to the place where I knew that if God chose for Kathy to die, I must be willing and accepting.

When you come to that point of ultimate relinquishment, peace comes. Perhaps that's why God gave me enough faith to hang in there with our daughter, no matter what medical experts said, no matter what the prognosis, no matter what we saw with our eyes. I did not have that faith, you understand; God provided it for me.

Even as I attended our comatose daughter, I was planning our future relationship. I would become her friend and confidante, rather than her "mom," with all that word connotes. Instead of being the kind of parent who smothered and controlled, I would follow Jesus' example. I would become her friend. Jesus said, "Henceforth I call you not servants . . . but I have called you friends . . ." (John 15:15).

While Jesus bore me up day to day, moment to moment, event to event, Larry had no such comfort. I ached to communicate some of my own peace to him, but I could not. You see, I had a full assurance from God that we were going to come into meaningful life, whatever that meant. I honestly didn't ask for a divine prognosis beyond that. If Kathy lived, and if she had to live in a wheelchair, I knew we'd have a good time in a wheelchair.

Larry's expectations for her were soundly based on medical experience and opinion. Bluntly, they gave us little or no hope. As the days and weeks stretched on, Larry experienced a growing concern for me that if Kathy died, or lived the rest of her life as a vegetable as the doctors expected, he'd then experience added heartbreak caused by a wife who insisted on being unrealistic. He expected me to have a breakdown.

How does a couple deal with such total noncommunication? I remember praying one night, after anguishing to see my husband's bitter weeping, "Lord, why can't You take some of this peace You've given me, and implant that in Larry? Why do You give me all the peace, and he is suffering?"

God showed me a mental picture of a traveler (me) in a foreign country, where nobody spoke any English. As I traveled, I never became angry at the people of that country because they couldn't speak my language. *Yes, Lord,* I thought. *You mean these messages of peace for me. This is Your word to me at this time. Larry does not yet speak Your language, so he can't understand when You speak to him. That's why he can't accept my explanations or believe the things You have spoken to my heart.*

Once I understood that, I couldn't stay frustrated by Larry's lack of faith. He simply did not yet speak the language. Still, how could I communicate with him, I wondered for the hundredth time. How could I help him? I felt like his coach, his mother, some sort of baby-sitter.

You are acting as a roadblock, the Lord told me. *You don't have to be any of those things. Just let Larry be. He can cry if he wants to cry.*

Of necessity, then, I relinquished Larry. We could no longer communicate, or seem to reach one another on any deep level. Even as I planned my future relationship to a daughter everyone thought was dying, I somehow relinquished my future with my husband, who was still very much alive—and raw with suffering.

Once we got Kathy home, our marriage seemed to worsen. There's no way to describe the unrelenting pressures Larry faced. Bills, phone calls, unfinished work, family needs, Kathy's slow progress, Larry Don's unfathomable behavior.... Only a very strong man could have handled all Larry did. But then, I'd always seen Larry as strong. I *expected* him now, more than ever, to perform from a position of strength, as he always had done. Where was his strength, when I so needed it?

Fortunately, I stayed so occupied with Kathy that I couldn't be tempted to pamper Larry. He had to handle his problems; I had to handle mine. From time to time I'd wonder, "Why isn't he ever here to hold me up?" Still, I never cried. I had no need to cry. I felt so thrilled at Kathy's every growth step—at the growth of new friendship and camaraderie between us....

Larry and I, by contrast, grew further and further apart. There were no harsh words or anger, but a wide separation between us—especially since his anger toward our son continued to escalate. No matter how hard I tried, I could not communicate to Larry that Larry Don had problems that anger never would solve.

I could see our son had an alcohol problem, a drug problem—or possibly both. I had grown up in a household where one parent was an alcoholic, and I knew the signs. I knew, but I could not convince Larry. He stayed constantly angry at Larry Don's behavior—the booze—the wrecked cars—yet he would not confront our son's true condition. Larry simply could not accept any possibility that his son might be an addict.

Though we occupied the same home, Larry and I nevertheless lived poles apart, as he dealt with one desperately needy child, I the other. Emotionally and physically, my husband and I experienced separation that seemed so deep, so inevitable, so *final.*

I missed Larry. I wanted that touching. I wanted to be cradled in his arms—comforted—loved. I missed all that terribly much. But I had come to believe that Larry no longer loved me, that our love was totally gone. When I thought of the distance between us—the mess our family was in. . . .

Ironically, as our marriage waned, our daughter began to flourish. God was giving us the miracle we had so earnestly claimed. Ever so slowly, Kathy progressed. Through the eyes of faith, I could see her totally—every bit whole!

What's more, even as Larry Don's behavior continued to worsen, I could see him healed also. I knew, from the bottom of my heart, that God would perform a miracle for our son, even as He had transformed our daughter.

I could not explain that to Larry, of course, any more than I had been able to explain what God had shown me concerning Kathy. Surely my vision of Larry Don—the boy people found so easy to love, so appealing, so irreplaceable in his own way—my stubborn vision of that boy's return would be termed "unrealistic." It certainly bore little resemblance to the surly, hurting, rebellious son with whom my husband had to deal so unsuccessfully.

That's where the book *Kathy* found us all. Our daughter had been restored to us. God performed a miracle in her behalf—in behalf of us all. We wrote the book to His glory, praying it might bless others as He had blessed us.

What a situation! Larry Miller had just turned forty, didn't like his job, wasn't sure where he was headed—a typical midlife crisis. And here I was, going out with Kathy from city to city, promoting a best-selling book, and leaving my husband at home to deal with a mixed-up son and financial stress. By now, to make things worse, profits from my Amway business were keeping us from losing our house. This was a lot for one man to handle. Larry had no comfort zone anywhere.

One day he drove Kathy and me to the airport and threw our luggage to the ground, obviously angry. On the plane I asked Kathy, "Help me figure out what that's all about. What's going on with Dad?"

"Mom, it's so apparent that he's jealous," she replied. "We're the ones who are going out, and he has to stay home and deal with stuff. Put yourself in his shoes. Wouldn't you be angry too?"

By this time, I was thinking if there were to be a divorce that I'd be the one to walk out, and that I had just cause. I felt Larry was totally to blame. I'd think, *Lord, I don't understand this. Here we've had this miracle, and You've given us this fine book, and I know You're working in Larry Don's life—that You will deliver him from drugs—and what about this marriage? It's going to smithereens!*

I'd also think to myself, *Here's a miracle story, on the one hand, but on the other hand, Barbara, you're going to walk out on this marriage. How can you say that's God's doing?*

That's when I recognized it was a satanic attack! If Satan couldn't kill us via Kathy's accident, or Larry Don's problems, he'd attack our marriage relationship and try to whack it off at the roots.

I began to claim our marriage would not fall apart. Now, I didn't know how it could come together, and by now I felt very little towards Larry. My love was packed away in a corner, because I had been neglected for a long, long time. If Larry Miller couldn't touch me and love me the way a man is supposed to love his wife, then I guess I didn't have to try to love him either.

Praise God! *The Lord did it.* The marriage got so bad, I simply had to turn loose. I came to the place where nothing mattered. I simply knew God was in charge; that He would make something happen. I surrendered Larry as first I'd relinquished Kathy, and later Larry Don.

A process began. It's a great mystery, something I cannot explain. It started with Kathy, as I tried to put into action toward her that nonjudgmental, unconditional love I wanted her to know. And when it worked with her, I tried it with Larry Don. Had I not tried hard to show them that sort of love, a love still foreign and "new" to me, I believe Larry Miller and I doubtless would be divorced today. I'd be divorced—and I wouldn't understand why.

What I need to stress here is, the process had to begin with *me.* God had provided *me* the tools, the training, the assurance. He expected me to use these tools so He could bless us all.

God's ways are far beyond our ways, His purposes beyond our purposes. Had our marriage felt comfortable to me, or had I understood myself at all, I might not have had the impetus to seek God in the first place. Also, had Larry comforted me as I wanted him to during Kathy's catastrophic problems, I might not have felt such a need for God.

I feel sure Kathy's recuperation period—those long weeks and months when I felt so distant, so estranged from the man I love—served as my wilderness experience, my time for drawing near to God, something He knew I needed.

Also, as a perceptive friend once pointed out, possibly the

sense of loss I felt regarding Larry, my grief about that chasm, that void, made me determined to fight with everything in me, in behalf of Kathy's life.

All these things are mysteries. We know very little, we understand almost nothing, about the marvelous workings of God. But Larry Miller and I know this much, at least: the Lord God of the universe has had His hand on our lives and on the Miller family, always.

Today we choose to make our marriage happy. It's wonderful to sit here at my desk, let my mind wander, and imagine how wonderful it will be when I see Larry in an hour or so. It's great, being held in his arms. It's wonderful to see him smile, to admire those strong shoulders and know how much they hold us all up. And it's wonderful to hold hands at the dining table, in the car, or as we climb into bed and offer up a prayer together to our Lord.

I'm so grateful for those simple things. They were absent in the past—those small things that all women long for. Yes, I also have a wealth of material things—all any woman would wish for. God, through my husband, has provided them all.

But what a woman *really* wants is that little touch of a hand, the pat on the shoulder, that phone call in the middle of the day: "Hi, Honey! I was thinking of you." Women don't hurt because they lack a vacation home, flashy jewelry, or furs. They hurt because they lack the tendernesses that only one man can give.

Sometimes, as I ponder these things—the amazing distance God has brought us from the way we were—I see Larry and Barbara, Larry Don and Kathy, from God's perspective.

Praise God forever!

10
Looking Ahead

Hi, there! I'm feeling great! Fantastic, excellent, just the best—that's the way I feel when I think about the things Mom just described. We really are a miracle family, aren't we? Larry Don and I feel fortunate that we've lived two different home lives the way we did. When we marry and have our own homes, we can look back on the example Dad and Mom set for us—people who're willing to work, willing to learn, willing to change. Above all, they didn't quit!

Looking through my journals, I see I refer to home so much. It's neat remembering how it felt to come home from the hospital. Soon after that, even with all she had to do for me during my rehabilitation, Mom and I began planning how to redecorate my room. She's a great one for keeping you looking ahead.

I'm really glad we live in Scottsdale. Arizona is such a beautiful place. I'm glad my dad decided to remain in Arizona when he retired from baseball, and that we got to grow up here.

Now that I'm about to be nineteen (Larry Don is three years older) I'm looking ahead to the kind of home I'll have someday. Mom and I talk about that a lot. She gives me some really profound thoughts on the subject; that where my life is today is my platform for where I'll be as a young married woman. That might be just a few years from now—who knows? When Mom was my age she was engaged, and she was only twenty when Larry Don came along. I doubt I'd want to get married quite that young, but I sure know quite a few girls who have.

In fact, I know girls my age who already have been married and divorced. I believe there's a grave danger that will happen when there's not good mother-daughter communication going for you.

Boy, do Mom and I communicate on *that* subject—marriage! When I reread my journals and realized how much I write about the guys, I decided I was boy crazy. Mom says that's normal at my age. In fact, she thinks it's a plus. Dad and Mom believe it's really good to know a lot about a lot of different guys, so I get some good ideas about the qualities I want and need to find in whomever I eventually marry.

The same goes for Larry Don. When he likes a young woman, I've noticed I'm apt to like her too, and so do Mom and Dad. Our parents want to know our friends. On the other hand, we want them to know our parents, because we're proud of our friends *and* our parents.

What about people who don't have all those good feelings between their parents and the guys or gals they happen to be dating? I say, if you're seeing someone who really is borderline and your parent objects, you're heading for trouble. Either you're going to sneak around and take sides with a guy who's up to no good, or you're going to accept your parent's opinions. With the teenagers I know, I think there's more friction over this one situation than almost anything else.

Sometimes I meet a girl my age (or even younger) who is

pregnant and unmarried. Usually those girls got into trouble with someone their parents didn't want them to see in the first place.

It makes you wonder. What in the world would they think of my father, who is so overprotective you wouldn't believe it? My father doesn't allow me to date any guy unless he first approves of him. That means he has to meet the guy, talk to him, and know what he's all about.

Someone said, "Isn't that hopelessly old-fashioned?"

"Old-fashioned, maybe," I said, "but not hopeless. It really takes the pressure off me. When my dad and mother think a young man is really neat, has fine qualities, it helps me a lot. For one thing, I never seem to go out with any losers!"

I like going out with guys my parents consider really nice, smart, considerate—all those good things. They're expecting me to end up with someone who is the cream of the crop. Most parents want that for their kids, but it takes some thought and experience before you know the kind of person you ought to marry. I believe the Lord will help me choose the right husband, but I've got to have the good sense to choose my companions wisely in the meantime.

As Mom describes throughout this book, the home I'm going to have someday will reflect a lot about the home I grew up in. Either I'll want my home to be a lot like hers, or I'll want the opposite. Knowing that, I can look around and appreciate Mom as a model for me. For example, take this entry in one of my journals:

> Hi! Today's been great. You know, I actually cooked the whole meal tonight by myself, with a little supervi-

sion from Mom. [This was when I was much younger.] It was absolutely fantastic!

Today was my dad's birthday, and we gave him a gold chain which he really loves. . . .

That was great training for me, right? Well, but we have to realize that not all girls are so privileged. In today's world, quite a few mothers work away from home, and many of my girl friends don't get a whole lot of chances for their mothers to teach them to cook, sew, or that sort of thing. What will those girls do two years from now, or five, when they have a home of their own to run?

It's my thinking that any young woman of eighteen or older sure needs to sit down with herself and figure out what she needs to learn before that big day happens. First, I believe, is knowing she's right with the Lord. I want Him to choose my husband, for sure!

A good way to get your thinking going along those lines is to start reading some Christian books about marriage. Or do like my mom did, and take a seminar that will help you know yourself as a woman. Anything that will get your thinking straight!

Mom has encouraged me this way for some time now. In one of my journals a couple of years ago I wrote:

I spent a whole day reading and writing a chapter report on a book Fleming H. Revell Company published, entitled *Intended for Pleasure,* by Dr. and Mrs. Wheat. Skimming the contents page, chapter 2 caught my eye, and I knew it's a really good chapter for me to read. It was on marriage counseling, and how God wants the best for us. . . .

Another thing, I believe kids really know those areas in which they're acting immature. I'd say, check the friction points. Where fathers and mothers are constantly on our backs about this problem or that, sometimes we spend all our time resisting our parents, instead of resisting the problem. If a girl is in her teens and constantly arguing with her dad and mom, in just a few years she'll be fussing with a husband.

If she gets herself into some Christian thinking, though, I believe she'll decide to love and submit to her parents. The Bible says in Ephesians 6:1: "Children, obey your parents in the Lord: for this is right."

Once we get down and do that, we ought to be mature enough to start training ourselves for the Big League stuff. Read Ephesians 5:22–33 and you'll see we have some heavy learning to do. Look it up. You'll love it!

God wants fathers and mothers to train their kids in how to take charge of their own lives, but these days a lot of kids are on their own, with very little training. It's really great to have strict parents, people who insist that you've got to measure up. I appreciate mine for that.

If you don't have that kind of parents, though, God still has answers for you. Even if you come out of a home where there's alcoholism, or divorce, or other serious problems, God can still train you and help you not to be held back by all that. He teaches us to look at the positives instead of the negatives. Our family really knows that from experience.

What should you do, in that case? Well, to the girls I meet when we're traveling—the ones who say, "If I just had a mom like yours, everything would be different"—all I can say is, God knows your situation. He loves you just as much as He loves me. He wants you to be happy. He wants to heal your emotions and your thinking and help you make a winner out of yourself, no matter what your home is like.

Where can you start? First, get into the Word of God. Get hold of a Bible that's easy for you to read and understand. Look for a church home where you can learn God's Word, get really great Bible teaching, and find good fellowship. Ask God to help you plug into the kind of Sunday-school class, or Bible study, or whatever kind of fellowship you need.

Also, I'd look for a Christian woman I could model myself after. You don't need to compare your mom, certainly, to other women. You don't need to tell her she doesn't measure up. You *do* need to let her know you love her!

But it's good—it's *excellent*—to get to know other older women you admire, women who can teach you, and begin to learn all you can about how to live a successful life.

One of the really beneficial effects about being a Christian is that we constantly learn from one another. You meet so many people with talents and skills who really feel honored to teach you what they know. And as you grow in your walk with Christ, you'll be that way, too—always looking for ways to be loving and giving.

I know many a girl who found Christ, changed herself and her way of living, and then her mom and dad accepted Jesus, just because of her example. I'd say, if you don't like the example your parents are setting for you, start setting a good Christian example for them! That's a good challenge for any kid by teen years' time.

Then, it's a good idea to look around at your friends— both girls and guys. I believe it's a good idea to go out with lots of different people. It broadens your thinking. Girls help other girls develop good taste, form opinions about ideas, clothes, home surroundings, all sorts of things. And when you date a number of different guys and become friends in a brother-sister way, it helps you decide what you really want in a man when the time comes for you to make that choice.

I'm really glad to have a brother as neat as Larry Don. Girls like him. He's good-looking, for one thing, but he can also be very sweet. He's good about helping me, and also encourages me, and even compliments me a lot. I admit we've been known to have our fusses, and he can be a real pain at times, but all in all I want to say anybody would be glad to have a brother like him. Between Dad and him I've already formed quite a few opinions about men!

The more people you get to know—whether they're your age or not—the more it helps you grow in different areas. I might not ever have realized that if my circumstances hadn't given me so many chances for travel and meeting new people. In fact, the "old" Kathy never did see my dad as anything but just my dad. It didn't occur to me it was possible to make friends with him; that someone that much older would be someone I'd want as a friend.

Now it's neat when we get to go out together, just the two of us, for lunch or a dinner date or something. I bet I'll think about that and remember those times, once I'm both grown *and* gone!

Our family's Amway business is one of the best reasons for helping me grow. It's the kind of business where you meet people from all over—people you'd never meet any other way—and all age groups at that. You're not just thrown with people your same age, but little kids and old people, as well as making friends with people your parents' age. All this is good experience for anybody. It's good training for marriage, when I'll have to adapt to my husband's friends and business associates.

To sum it all up, it's exciting to be looking forward to marriage someday soon—and to be getting ready for adult life. We should be enjoying ourselves a lot. Why is it so many people our age feel miserable?

You know the answer to that. They're not facing their life, trying to make something out of it that's really good. Instead they're smoking pot, skipping school, doing all these things they think are really cool—but aren't.

The Lord will help us turn it all around. For any girl my age or even quite a bit younger, I think it's a good idea to make a list of questions—a checklist for yourself. Maybe you'd want to keep the questions just to yourself, or maybe you'd want to discuss them with adults you respect.

Here are some of the questions I think kids our age need to find answers for:

1. Do I believe in God? Am I saved? Do I really know how to get right with God, and am I ready to put my life in His hands?

2. Where do I stand with my parents? If I am in poor fellowship with them, how can I improve that relationship? Maybe you can talk that question over with your dad and mom. If things are really bad, maybe you should talk to your pastor, academic advisor, or some other person who could give excellent help. Above all, talk to the Lord about it!

3. What kind of people do I know? Do I choose to know people who waste time and obviously want to

become losers? Do I have friends who are serious about their life and their future?

4. What kind of example do I set? Do I have high standards, or do I prefer to be a slob?

5. What kind of reputation am I making for myself? Am I the kind of girl who will be an asset to a guy— somebody he's proud to take out?

6. Do I think, talk, and act like a representative of Jesus Christ?

7. Do I dress nicely? Am I neat and ladylike? Do I like my looks and enjoy my personality? All of these can be changed, with a little guidance. There are plenty of good books and courses to help.

8. What kind of guys do I choose to date? Am I going out with young men who would be very poor marriage risks? If so, what a waste of time. You'll either fail to know the kind of guys you *would* like to marry someday, or you'll run the risk of falling in love and marrying a real loser.

9. What would my father and my mother advise me about marriage someday? What kind of man do they hope I'll marry? What mistakes have they made in marriage they hope I can avoid? Ask them. You might be surprised at what they'll say. I'm sure they're very interested in who you will bring into the family some-day, and I know they want you to be happy.

10. What couples do I know who have really good marriages, and what makes them work? Why are their homes so happy?

Those questions are just for starters. You might be thinking you're too young to ask them, but I bet you're not.

One thing sure, I believe God wants us to study life and try to make the best of it. He wants to guide our future and make it excellent—super—fantastic—just the very best. Praise God!

11
Father and Son

The air suddenly filled with profanities as my nineteen-year-old son loped across our yard, yelling for me as he ran. "Mom, come here! I've really messed up now!"

What in the world could Larry Don have done this time? I wondered. *At ten in the morning, surely he isn't already into booze or drugs!*

I hurried outside to where he and his friend Mark surveyed the car they'd been driving to the airport. One glance at the vehicle, with its entire front end shoved into a crumpled, bizarre-looking slant, and I felt sick. *Another wrecked automobile! A bad wreck, too—it could have killed both boys. Thank You, Lord—but dear God, what will Larry do about this?*

Apprehension swept over me in waves, as I steadied myself and tried to think what to do and say. Larry would be livid. The friction between Larry Don and his father had reached unbearable levels lately. My instincts told me this newest near-fatal accident would pile the final straw on Larry's emotional load.

Larry Don had the same thoughts, apparently. Morose and dejected, head down and body slumped, he gazed at the wreckage unbelievingly, muttering an occasional obscenity for whatever comfort it might offer. Mark stood by, mute

119

and apparently okay. Larry Don also appeared untouched except that his slender body trembled from head to toe.

I began to pray silently—a quick, emergency prayer. Then I took my son's hand and said, "I want you to agree with me in prayer about this situation." Both boys seemed too dazed and distraught to resist, so I launched into a strong, firm prayer, asking God to handle this mess, and telling Him we were agreeing with Him for a healing.

My son was so afraid to tell his father what he had done. "Larry Don, we're going to claim that God has the answer," I told him. "I don't know how your father will react to this, but it's going to be okay. Trust God with this situation."

My own trust seemed to falter, however, as Larry Don returned to the car to drive Mark to the airport, and I turned toward our house, preparing myself to phone Larry at work. I wanted to give Larry Don's father the bad news, rather than have him do it.

That seemed to be our pattern these days. It was always Barbara who acted as mediator, who tried to act as family pacifist. *What other choice do I have?* I asked myself for the millionth time. The father-son relationship had become explosive. This phone call I had to make would be equivalent to throwing a lighted match into a gasoline tank, so obviously I must be the one to place it, no matter how much I dreaded to do so.

At that point, two years after Kathy's terrible experience, Larry Miller seemed simply unable to absorb any further trauma. He felt so battered already. Would Kathy progress any further? Would she attain anything resembling normalcy, or would he be supporting a semifunctional daughter the rest of his life? He was trying to handle those questions, deal with a pressure job, continue in a marriage that had lost its vitality. . . .

He didn't need this. Larry couldn't handle Larry Don because he himself was zapped. That's why, when I attempted to discuss our problems concerning our son, Larry always refused to admit there *was* a problem.

Now, silently, half praying and half arguing with myself, I looked at our dilemma one more time, as I prepared to dial Larry's office number. The facts were stark: I'd been picking up on Larry Don's signals because I'd grown up with an alcoholic father, and had an alcoholic grandfather as well. I'd sought the Lord so many times, asking Him to show me in my spirit if Larry Don's behavior pattern reflected what I'd known in my earlier life. How could we ignore these continual signs?

I could see Larry Don was headed for death. He had discussed suicide with me. He had walked away from so many minor automobile accidents, had totaled four cars.

I rang through to Larry and began a crisp, factual recitation of the facts. They had approached an intersection; Larry Don had looked to his left, expecting Mark to look to the right, to make sure all was clear, but as Larry Don entered the intersection, a car approaching from their right slammed to a halt, then skidded into the boys' vehicle.

Larry became incensed at the news. Even as we spoke, however, another call came in—this one from the man who had hit Larry Don's car. Our son's bad driving caused the accident, the man informed my husband.

That unpleasant duty done, I returned to the family room and got alone with the Lord. I felt such desolation, such fear. "Lord, I really don't know what else to do," I confessed.

"I'm at my wit's end. I just want to thank You in advance that You have a healing for Larry Don through drug rehabilitation.

"You see, I can't go any further, and I can't ask You to take me any further. I feel he has a sickness—surely if it were something we could define, we'd get help for him. *Please give me strength to find my son some help.*"

Actually, I'd already found the place where Larry Don Miller could receive the help he needed—a very fine facility called The Meadows, some eighty miles from our Scottsdale home. Two weeks earlier, in fact, I'd turned over all the data to one of my best friends, who had just recognized that her son needed help for his drug addiction. When her son was admitted to The Meadows, the Lord told me that our son would be next.

There in our family room, two weeks later, I was weeping and saying, "Thank You, Lord. Your promise is real, and this is the time."

Immediately I went to the telephone and contacted the intervention counselor in our community. I told him I knew our son had a problem, and I had reached the end of my tolerance. No longer could I act as though there were nothing wrong, nor could I continue to make excuses for his destructive behavior. Although Larry still could not bear the thought that his son might be addicted, I could no longer stand the burden. I had to have an appointment.

We set a time for the following day. I felt so excited, so hopeful, that my heart literally sang. Once again I went before the Lord, this time with prayers of thanks and praise.

It was hours before Larry Don returned home, but God gave me peace even about that. When he came in, I looked into his tight, closed, vulnerable young face and said, "I have no idea where you went or what you did after you took Mark to the airport, but I'll tell you what I would have done if I had been in your shoes."

He looked up, surprised, and I continued. "If I had been you, I would have smoked some grass, or popped a pill— used some kind of chemical—some mood-altering drug. . . ."

At that, Larry Don began to cry. "Son," I told him as I fought my own tears, "I see a very sick person before me. If you had cancer, a broken bone, or kidney problems, we'd spare no expense to find you the best medical help available. I believe you have a drug problem and an alcohol problem. We're going to get you the finest help available, and you're going to be healed."

I spoke with conviction, and when I told him about the appointment I'd set up for the next day, he readily agreed to the counseling. My heart filled with relief and gratitude, as I realized *it had been so easy.* I didn't *tell* him he must go; I *asked* him—and he agreed. I guess I knew he'd agree, because God had told me he would.

Larry, Sr., however, presented a real challenge. He came home, furious, exploding over the latest in a string of baffling, embarrassing episodes. This one touched off another battle, so it was well after dinner before I had an opportunity to sit down with Larry to discuss the appointment I'd arranged for the next day.

"No way," he replied heatedly. "We can't afford it. We're still in debt from Kathy's medical bills. . . ."

I broke into his hostile response. "Larry, money is no problem," I began.

"No problem!" He stared at me angrily.

"God owns everything in the world," I continued calmly.

"And He has shown me that lack of money is not what's standing in the way of our helping Larry Don.

"That's your cop-out, Larry," I said wearily. "I love you, and I know God can speak to you and tell you what to do for our son. I've prayed so much, I *know* this is what we must do. If you can't bring yourself to do it, you'll just have to let God deal with you the best way He can!"

Feeling unbelievably tired, I took myself to bed. *What will Larry decide?* I wondered briefly. Well, I'd just have to leave him in God's hands. As for my own decision, it was firmly set. I'd take my son for the counseling he so desperately needed. It might save his life.

The next morning Larry Don drove us to the counselor's office. He was angry and speeding, driving with jerky impatience, because he knew he needed to go but he didn't want to go at all. Then we arrived to find that Larry was not there. Disappointed, I prayed, "Thank You, anyhow, Lord. I know You're taking care of our situation." Then Larry arrived. He was ten minutes late, but he arrived.

The three of us entered the counselor's office as a team. Larry's interviewer, himself a recovering alcoholic, immediately put us at ease. "No matter what this young man has done, no matter how bad it might be, it's all been done before," he reminded us. "He hasn't invented anything new." We felt ourselves relax as he turned to Larry Don.

"What *have* you done?" he queried. "Why don't you start at the beginning and tell us everything?"

It was as though suddenly the dam broke, as Larry Don sat and confessed his destructive acts. Larry and I sat dumbfounded. You could see the closed, surly expression our son had worn into the room replaced by relief and release, then a beautiful look of hope and peace.

Larry Don never before had had occasion for such a confession. He told it all. You could see the shock waves hit his father, for Larry truly had no idea of the dimension of our son's problems. This session tore him up.

Nevertheless, it became painfully clear that Larry Don needed to admit himself to The Meadows. Miraculously, there was an opening on Wednesday of that very week. That piece of news made hope rise full force within my heart, but then I heard our son say there was no way he could be ready that early. He must make job arrangements; he must do this and that. It was a put-off, but something inside me said, *Let him do this his way. Leave him his dignity.* He decided to enter The Meadows on Saturday.

By Friday evening, Larry and I felt great heaviness in our spirits. We didn't speak of it, but it was there—a grief, a sadness, at what we had to do the next day. We felt very tired, and went to bed early, only to be awakened at five the next morning by loud knocking at our front door. Larry jumped out of bed. I followed him down the hall, and through the Plexiglas pane beside the door I saw a flashlight and the silhouette of a police officer.

"Sir, do you own a car with license number ————?" the officer inquired.

"Yes, we do."

"Do you know where the driver is?"

"No. It's our son. Can you tell us what's wrong?"

We learned that there had been a hit-and-run accident. It didn't involve persons, but property damage. There in the dark, I could almost see the steam rising in Larry. His voice grew strained and hostile, as he questioned the officers. They said it was imperative that we try to locate Larry. If we could get him to the police station before half-past nine the next morning, they would not issue a warrant for his arrest.

What could we do? Not knowing where to begin to look for him, we hurriedly began dressing so we could begin our search. It occurred to me that Larry Don might be taking refuge at his friend's house, but when I phoned there the friend had not seen him. As I turned toward our bedroom, I thought I'd turn on the light in Larry Don's room, so I could better tell when he entered. As I walked over to the light, I tripped across our son.

He had passed out and was sound asleep on the floor. Wearing a pair of pajamas we'd bought for The Meadows, he looked for an instant like the sweet, uncomplicated youngster we'd so loved and enjoyed. I picked him up, just like a little baby. He's bigger than I, and I couldn't carry him, but I somehow got him into bed, all the time chiding him as though he were a small child. I ordered him to stay in bed, told him if he got out I'd whip him. Impossible! He was too out of it to know that, of course, and he did stay put.

By breakfast time, Larry was furious. He wasn't taking Larry Don to the police station—*he* was going to work. He was all worked up; he couldn't face one more thing. So I got Larry Don out of bed and told him we had to go to the police station, and he had to turn himself in. He was so scared he looked literally sick.

"I've prayed about it," I said, trying to make my voice stop shaking. "Just be truthful. Whatever you do, be honest with these men. If you're honest, God can protect you."

He told me his story on the way to the station. He had decided to have one last fling, he said. The day before he felt so afraid, just sheer fear that he would die before he got the help he needed. After work, he had attended a party where he got good and high. When he left for home, driving that car he'd wrecked earlier in the week, he took a back street so he'd be less conspicuous. The car had been knocked so cockeyed that the lights pointed not straight ahead but to the left. He didn't want to see any policemen, in his condition.

The weird lights prevented him from seeing a fence along that unfamiliar street, so he hit it. Not only did he take down a whole row of chain link fence, but it tore up what was left of his car, threw Larry Don forward against the steering wheel and momentarily stunned him.

He reversed the automobile and started limping towards home—a difficult feat, since he was driving a vehicle with three blown-out tires. He was creeping along at three o'clock in the morning, trying not to attract attention, with sparks flying from the wheel rims, when he saw a car following him. Thinking it might be the police, Larry Don eased over into a parking lot and stopped. The other car stopped, too, and a man got out and approached him.

"I don't know where your head is," the gentleman said, "but I know what it feels like to be your father. I've had three sons who are just like you. I've been through that pain three times.

"You get in my car. I'm taking you home."

To this day, I know that anonymous, compassionate father as an angel, unaware. He took Larry Don home, where he passed out on the floor. It's a miracle, too, that we had no knowledge he was there; otherwise, we would have had to turn him over to the police.

At the police station Larry was very honest. He told them

he had a drug and alcohol problem and was to be admitted to The Meadows at noon that day. He had to pay a fine, but they let him go. They could have thrown the book at him!

Before we left, we asked to look at Larry Don's impounded car. Unbelievable! The fenders were gone, the mirror gone, all tires gone except for a few shreds of rubber remaining on one wheel. The vehicle looked threadbare. I walked away heavyhearted, but with a curious realization that God's hand was so strong on our son's life *that very day*—and that if we needed further confirmation about the necessity for his entering The Meadows, this was it!

Within hours, Larry and I had accompanied Larry Don to his destination. It was a hard time for us. We knew we were leaving him in good hands, but it hurt.

Larry Don often has said that one of the greatest releases he ever experienced was to sit before his parents and enumerate all the wrong things he had done. He had been so sneaky, so defensive, about his life. Now he was laying it bare; the very worst was known.

Had Larry not heard these things from our son's lips, he perhaps could not have been reconciled to leaving the young man at The Meadows. That day I saw my husband as a man who felt heavyhearted beyond description, but acknowledging that we had to do a very hard thing.

Watching him drive, a mixture of stark love and pain written across his face, my heart went out to Larry as it never had before.

Kathy and Larry Don pose in front of the beautiful Arizona landscape before hiking into Havasupai Canyon.

Kathy and Dr. Robert Schuller after her appearance on his "Hour of Power" program. *Left:* Kathy is introduced with Charles Paul Conn, coauthor of the book *Kathy.* The two have appeared at many Amway conventions as well as such functions as this one: The Bob Crisp Family Reunion '80 in Chicago.

Larry Don and Kathy on the way to the Bob Crisp Family Reunion '81.

Since her own life has been touched by physical tragedy, Kathy has a special feeling for the handicapped. Here she talks to Joni Eareckson at CBA (Christian Bookseller's Association) in Dallas. Joni has been paralyzed from the neck down since a diving accident. *Below:* Senator Ted Kennedy and son Teddy, Jr. (back to camera) talk to the Millers in London, where Kathy received the International Award for Valour in Sport. Young Kennedy's leg was amputated at the knee to prevent the spread of bone cancer.

Promoting *Kathy* took Kathy and her mother not only to the CBA convention but all over the United States. They met wonderful people everywhere. *Below:* Kathy poses at CBA with two other well-known authors: Marabel (*Total Woman*) Morgan and Dale Evans Rogers (*Angel Unaware, The Woman at the Well, Woman,* and many other best-sellers).

Doris Barlow is pictured here with Kathy and (front row) Gordon
Barlow (Barbara's brother) and his sons Brad (on lap) and Gordon.
Below: The Millers' good friend Dick Dennis found the now-
famous "I'm Gonna Win" tee shirt. Here some of Kathy's Salt Lake
City admirers sport the shirt that became Kathy's comeback
symbol.

Kathy wears the famous shirt to meet Art Linkletter as Barbara looks on. *Left:* Their love and marriage renewed, Barbara and Larry Miller had "stayed in the race," as Barbara writes.

Barbara walks into the garage to find Larry's surprise birthday present to her on the Big Fortieth: a sea-green sports convertible, wrapped in red ribbons. *Below:* The end of a movie, not the end of the story. Kathy and Barbara listen carefully as the final night of filming for the television version of *Kathy* comes to an end. It was the last scene, in which Larry Don and his dad make up after a quarrel. When this picture was taken, it was after 1:00 A.M., very cold—and very emotional for both Kathy and Barbara.

12

Free Indeed

I'm taking my child to The Meadows because he needs help, the parent thinks. *I'm taking my child to get him fixed. This child is causing all our problems. If we can get him fixed, our problems will be gone. . . .*

At The Meadows, they feature something called Family Week. When a patient's therapy progresses to a certain point, the staff calls in the rest of his family for group sessions. We arranged to take a week's vacation for that purpose, and traveled to The Meadows wonderfully prepared to help Larry Don.

I'd been warned to expect quite an experience. When one of my friends returned from Family Week, in fact, she telephoned our house, simply babbling.

"You've got your head messed up," I told her. "What in the world did you let them do to you?"

So I went there thinking, *God is going with us, and we're going to be a big help to Larry Don.* I knew we had Christ, so they couldn't mess up our heads. Almost immediately, however, I saw that indeed we did have Christ—but our family was dysfunctional anyhow. We had a lot to learn!

In one week of intensive therapy a family can travel a tremendous distance. I found our experience to be the most intense work I'd ever experienced. On Day One, which they call Depot Day, we found ourselves sitting at the "bus stop," observing the other "passengers," sizing them all up. It's a polite moment. Everybody says who they are (not why they are there, but who they are). That moment marked the beginning of a very painful five-day trip.

With the families of other patients, we learned about ourselves, our families, and *their* families. Morning sessions included our "family group" (the individuals I just listed), and were led by counselors skilled in group therapy .

You share, and others mirror what they hear you saying. They see things you won't even tell them, but the moment you're caught in their cross fire, you know what they're saying is true. If you try to deny it, it becomes even more uncomfortable. Just as I had begun to be acquainted with the dynamics of this often-painful sharing, something happened that nearly wiped me out.

"Barbara," a counselor asked, "I wonder why, in your book *Kathy,* you said, 'Kathy simply stepped into the path of a car.' Why were you so protective of the driver? Why were you not accusing?"

I felt a strange sort of agitation as I framed my careful answer. "I . . . I deliberately phrased it that way. I didn't want the driver to feel responsible. It was an accident. He didn't mean to do it."

Dead silence. I caught my breath, wondering why I felt so defenseless . . . so . . . *on the spot.*

"No, that's not true," the counselor replied. "The reason you phrased it that way is, *you knew she purposely walked in front of the car.*"

His words struck me like so many bullets. Larry stared at me—simply stared—disbelief written all over his face. I could feel him feeling with me, see him wondering how I would respond.

There was only one response possible, of course. "It's true," I whispered. "Three weeks before that automobile struck Kathy, she almost got hit by another car."

Tears rained down my face, just as they had eighteen months earlier, when God brought to my memory that scene with the angry lady who warned Kathy—who warned us all—about a young girl's carelessness, and where it might tragically lead.

As I told Larry Don's "family" the entire story, the rest of the Miller family heard it from my lips for the first time. And as I recounted that stirring, horrifying episode, I accepted our counselor's statement as truth. It became plain to me. I felt it. I could not deny it.

In fact, I realized, Kathy *had* almost deliberately walked in front of that car—not as a conscious plan, to make problems—but simply the unthinking act committed by a child preoccupied with her own hurt—a child who hurts because she doesn't see in her home the love that needs to be there— a child who doesn't know what's wrong at home, just that something *is* wrong—a child who becomes careless because nothing seems to matter, since there is not quite enough love to go around.

Despite the pools of tears in my eyes, I "saw" more clearly at that moment than ever before. I saw with spiritual eyes, because God allowed me to accept reality like a lightning flash. *Kathy's accident had not produced the problems in our home.* Her accident had happened because we had a dysfunctional, unbalanced family. I saw that and much, much more; far more than I could articulate through my painful sobs.

And I saw Larry. I saw the shocked, compassionate look on my husband's face, as he tried to absorb the truths just exploded in that room.

There was much more to come, that week. I came to understand how my actions during Larry's identity search, when I had taken over in his stead, had emasculated my husband's ego. Since he didn't seem to know where he was going with his life, I became the comforter, the rescuer. I took over completely. And since I assumed the position of supermom, Larry simply had no need to act as the man of our household.

A disturbed husband-wife relationship also disturbs the children, so I learned how Kathy became the rescuer who by her subconscious and near-fatal action provided the means of pulling our family together. Larry Don, meanwhile, in an attempt to find his own way of receiving love and attention, developed a death wish. After all, how do you top your sister's ten-week coma?

Larry Don lost a handful of close friends in teenage fatalities. Sensitive as he is, he suffered additionally in behalf of the loved ones involved. Suicide, therefore, seemed unthinkable to Larry Don. A car accident, however, something nondeliberate, unpremeditated—*that* would be different.

I thought of all the times our son had stated that he didn't care whether he lived or died. I also remembered all the ways he *showed* he didn't care.

It hurt to remember the days when, engrossed in Kathy's life-and-death struggle, we stayed at the hospital day and night. I tried so hard to spread myself to include our teenage son. I took pains to be home with him at the dinner hour, tried hard to nurture him properly, yet he still felt deeply lonely and left out. He needed his family. He couldn't handle the fear of his sister's death, the guilt he felt, the strangeness of it all.

Larry Don learned he could depend on alcohol and drugs. They became his family and they were always there; they never let him down. He turned to chemicals, which in turn produced guilt, which led him to subconscious suicide efforts—a cycle Satan clearly inspired.

Now we began to see ourselves as a very disjointed family, with many people hurting. Larry, Larry Don, Kathy, and I experienced much pain during Family Week, as did the others, but thank God we stuck with it. We saw we had begun a journey where Christ could heal each of us as individuals. And when the individuals were healed, the family could be put back together again.

Each of us began to see how much we yearned to come together as a family.

Before that could happen, however, we had to face a day that seemed particularly difficult; something The Meadows calls "Stuck Day." That morning's assignment is for each person to determine where he is "stuck." Why would you want your patient *not* to get well? How does his illness benefit you?

On the face of it, it might seem ridiculous. Why would we be there at all, unless we wanted Larry Don healed? But as the Bible says, we are "fearfully and wonderfully made." Skillful questioning revealed what Kathy might have to gain by Larry Don's continuing struggles: she could continue in her role as "good child" while he, typecast as the "bad child," provided contrast.

When it came Barbara Miller's turn to learn why I was "stuck," I felt that same anguished shock I'd felt that long-ago day in my car. I can hardly bear to remember the pain I felt at discovering that *Larry Don represented, to me, my alcoholic father.*

Insecure in my failing marriage, through Larry Don I had determined to hang on to my father. *I never had given away my dad.* Reeling with the force of that idea, trying to absorb the fact of what I unintentionally had done to my son, I heard the counselor suggest that I return for a second round of "Family Week." At that time, he said, I could work through my relationship to my father.

Emotionally exhausted, the three Millers who had so cheerfully offered to come help Larry Don found themselves departing for home—talked out, cried out, completely worn-out! And at home, in prayer, I knew our counselor was right. I must return to The Meadows on Monday. I must begin the hard grief work I had avoided since my father's death.

I was to struggle with my father for two long, intense days. I had to choose someone to serve as proxy for my dead daddy, so we could stage a "burial." It was very revealing.

It's uncanny how much the man I chose to play "dad" actually looked like my father. Stretched out on the sofa, the lights dimmed, he, indeed, looked "dead" to the three of us—Larry Don, Kathy and myself—seated on chairs before the "coffin." Larry Don's group of patients, with a couple of other people the Lord had impressed me to invite, served as our support group.

"Barbara, how did you feel when you learned about your father's death?" the counselor's kind voice asked. I described my feelings, the subsequent flight to where my father's funeral service would be solemnized, even went on to describe the funeral home, the way my father looked, the room where his body lay.

"Tell your father about the good moments and other good things you want him to know," the quiet voice instructed me. I leaned toward the immobile figure on the sofa. "Dad," I began haltingly, "remember when we children were 'good,' and you'd take us to the thirty-one-flavors store for ice cream—and you'd *always* get plain old vanilla?

"It was such fun when we'd coax you to take us to the circus. That was so special . . . and when you spent a dollar on that chameleon, and Mom was so furious! Dad, when I started to date . . . and you gave the boys' cars the once-over, and if they didn't look pretty good, you wouldn't let 'em park in our driveway!

"I remember how wonderful it was to bring Larry home. You really liked him, and it thrilled me that you'd watch television together, or Larry would help you with the barbecue grill. You'd shoot the breeze about sports together, and I'd watch you. I was so in love, and it meant so much that you loved Larry, too!

"Thanks, Dad, that you and Mom drove all the way from Kansas City the night Larry Don was born. You sat up all night long in the cold waiting room to greet your new grandson! Then you hurried back and bragged so much about the baby that it got written up in the company newspaper!

"And Dad, I remember hugging you around your middle. You were so big I couldn't reach all the way around—but it felt so good. You were so big and loving, so giving, so touching. I'd always side with you in those family battles. Honestly, Dad, Mom was such a nag!" On and on it came, the memories fresh, painful—and healing.

"Now tell your father about the disappointments and heartaches," I heard. Gulping, forcing back hard tears, I complied. It's unreal how you're *there,* back at age seven, wailing with pain. For the first time ever, I confronted my father with the hurts I'd felt all my life. I told him about the times he didn't come—the disgust I felt when he was drinking—the disappointments he caused me to feel—every bit of it.

"Barbara, tell your father how much you loved him," the compassionate voice encouraged me. "And tell him how he affected your life." I almost fell apart with weeping.

"Because I haven't relinquished you—I kept you alive in my son. His drinking has been . . . comfortable . . . to me, because I rescued him—just like I used to rescue you."

"Tell your father what you're going to do about that."

"It's going to stop this moment," I said, feeling new strength and hope rise in me. "You're not going to be part of my life anymore. You're dead, and you're fine, and you're with the Lord.

"Dad, you're not taking part in today, in the here and now. From now on you won't influence our lives. I'm giving Larry Don his freedom. He no longer has to serve as your image for me."

"Say your farewell to your father," the counselor said.

Then came a beautiful time of crying and being able to say, "I know you're in heaven and I'll see you again some day. I don't have to hang on to you now."

"Close your eyes now, Barbara, and say a prayer for your father," my counselor instructed.

When I opened my eyes, the proxy had left. The sofa was empty. "What do you see, Barbara?"

"My father is gone."

"What do you feel now?"

"I hurt. I feel very lonely. [All of which I had not felt, when my dad actually died.] I feel really sad my dad is gone and I won't see him again. It hurts to know I can't see him until I meet him in heaven."

"That's what you're supposed to feel," he responded, as he stepped forward and hugged me. "I'm very sorry, Barbara, that you lost your father. I'm very sad that he won't be a part of your life. I'm sad he won't see your children grow up; that was important to you. But I want you to know he is with God, and that gives us great comfort."

Every person in the room crowded around, hugged me and cried with me, and they were my family. Each told me how sorry he was, and then we were three—Larry Don, Kathy and me. I embraced my kids, one at a time, and told them I felt so sorry their grandfather would never get to see them and do the things grandfathers get to do with their kids.

"Will you forgive me?" I asked Larry Don, as he wrapped his arms around me in a strong, loving hug. "Will you forgive me that I allowed my dad's drinking to exist in you, to keep him alive? Will you forgive me that I didn't give *you* the room you needed?"

"Yes, Mom. I forgive you," he said over and over, and I heard *freedom* in his voice.

"I want more than anything else in the world for you to be well. I'd do anything for you to have your freedom," I told him. "I want you to know you're not my father any more. We're going to fight to get you well!"

Now that I had the freedom that comes only with an inner healing, my next desire was to call Larry (in Phoenix at work) to share my joy and begin our relationship anew!

Larry Don stayed eight weeks at The Meadows, trying hard to free himself from his addiction. He returned home clean and straight. We felt so proud of him, so thrilled at his recovery, yet some instinct within me said the healing was not yet complete—that even this change would not last.

Within two or three weeks, Larry Don slipped back into his old way of life. Today Larry and I realize that we had not claimed, had not even expected, a miracle for our son from Jesus Christ. Instead, we were skeptical, watching for him to slip—and he did. It hurts to admit that we did not wage the same spiritual warfare in his behalf that we had for Kathy. Had we ever *expected* her to slip back, we would have lost her.

Larry Don's healing came in May 1981, when he accepted Jesus Christ as his Lord and Savior. That time none of us questioned the transaction. We saw him healed. It showed in his radiant face, his buoyant spirit, his freedom of mind, body, and personality. Praise the Lord!

Today Larry Don is a prince. It was fun to see the change in him. He demonstrates compassion, tenderness, and shows so much caring. The four-letter words are gone, replaced by consideration and kindness. His manner is so loving. The Lord placed a beautiful spirit in our son.

One big thrill God gave me with this new person in Christ was to sit down and have Bible study with him. It still amazes me to see this young man avidly reading God's Word each day, as Kathy does.

He does so many other little things he never did before. He'll wash the car, trim the hedge, take out the trash and such helps without being asked.

However, it's in his relationship to his father that God demonstrated the most dramatic, tangible change of all.

With his new spiritual eyes, Larry Don perceived his father's needs. He was the one who said, "Mom, we need to pray for Dad." So the three of us joined in prayer for his dad, that Larry could turn everything in his life over to Jesus Christ and become free at last.

I'm convinced that the eight weeks our son invested at The Meadows was not so much for him as for our family as a whole. He worked hard, but at that time had no personal knowledge of Jesus Christ. Without Jesus, he lacked the power it takes to effect a lasting change.

I went there armed with the strength of our Lord. When trained workers offered the *why* of our family's behavior patterns, I had Jesus to help me change myself. Once you have the tools, the motivation and Christ to supply the power, you possess the means for correcting any defeating types of behavior.

Would I advise other families like ours to seek such counseling? Absolutely, within these considerations:

1. *Praise the Lord.* Thank Him in advance for the answer to your situation and confirm in prayer that He will direct you to the proper counselor. *Seek a Christian counselor* who can apply God's perspective to your life.

2. *Be willing to work.* In fact, Larry says you may even have to be willing to be willing! Counseling and therapy represent hard work, as we learned, but Larry and I were to discover that our willingness to help Larry Don eventuated in a resurrected marriage—for us!

Without The Meadows, I truly believe our marriage would have ended in divorce. I would have said, "Lord, what went wrong? I was such a good person, Lord, and I tried so hard. What went wrong?" I might never have understood such an outcome.

Fortunately, counseling opened some doors for us and enabled us to function as a healthy family. We also now know how to relate well to other people, and I'm able to help my extended family, brother and sisters, as well as friends, unlock some doors in their own lives.

I left The Meadows knowing I had victory in Christ. I understood where I fit into my childhood family. I understood my behavior as a child; understood why that behavior no longer had to threaten me as an adult; understood how I was off balance with my current family, and how I could get back into balance.

I also knew that regardless of the future situations which may arise in our lives, with God's help, we'll make it through. As the psalmist says:

> For by thee I have run through a troop; and by my God have I leaped over a wall.
>
> Psalms 18:29

God offers that same victorious life-style to all who seek Him for it. How Larry and I praise Him, that today we have the tools we need, the understanding, and most of all, Christ Himself to lead us through.

The Son has set us free, and we are free indeed!

13
Feelings

What a great day this is! Everything is beautiful. I feel like hugging the world!

Mom taught me to put my feelings down on paper. While I was in rehabilitation, when it took so much effort to talk, it seemed I could sort things out by writing. Now recording my feelings that way just comes naturally. You should see my tall stack of *feelin'* books!

Those days, my emotions got tangled up a lot. Many times I felt frustrated and angry. I knew I was different from other kids my age, and somehow I had to work that out. One example: being in a wheelchair in public; seeing people walk right past and not speak—just ignore me.

When that happened, I'd feel so frustrated and hurt. I wanted to stand up and yell, "Hey, see me? Look at me. Kathy Miller is here!"

As Mom explained, it's hard for some people to handle those who are different. Dad and Mom took me everyplace with them in those days, so I saw many hundreds of people—but it seemed like so few saw me. Most looked away.

In my heart I did not believe Kathy always would be in that chair—but there was a chance. Right away we noticed two kinds of people—those who stared, and those who quickly

149

.

looked away. It was rare for someone to stop and speak, to treat her normally.

That taught me something. If people had come up and talked to me, maybe touched or caressed me, that would have helped. I felt so lonely.

Of course, I knew God was with me, but I was lonely for people. I had a lot of time to spend with God in those days. Later He got me out of that wheelchair for good, but I hope I always remember my feelings, so I can empathize with people who are different, or old, or maybe neglected little kids.

Kathy and I often say we feel very strongly that there are too few "touchers" in the world. Maybe we're out to change that a little bit. I've always loved hugs, pats, and kisses, but Kathy's accident changed our whole family into touchers. We learned the healing power of the human touch—especially in a fragile situation.

While Kathy was in a coma, I felt very strongly that her inner spirit was able to "hear," so I allowed no negatives to enter her room. At the same time, I believed she could feel our touches. I began to do some things other people thought were rather strange. I wanted her to feel loved.

Mom knew I always took good care of my hair and skin, so two or three times a week she would shampoo my hair, blow dry it, and style it different ways. I didn't know anything about it, of course. She also gave me facials once or twice a week, and gave me massages. It must have felt wonderful.

I'd touch her every time I talked to her. I'd say, "Honey, there has been an accident; you're in the hospital, and your body is healing. I don't want you to be afraid. Everything will be fine."

Larry Don touched Kathy a lot, too. Her accident threw her so far across the pavement that she had abrasions on her face, arms and legs. Larry Don rubbed Vitamin E oil into every injury, so today there's hardly a scar on Kathy's body. I tell him he loved her scars away. His touching and concern showed how much he really cared.

I don't think we should wait until someone is in a coma! When a mother and a child are having difficulties, or when someone is in a snit for some reason, even when we can't get our love message across in words, we can touch the other person in a loving way. Touching is communication. It reassures me. When words won't help, touching will.

Your behavior shouldn't have anything to do with it. A hug, to me, means *I love you,* whether you love my behavior or not. When Larry Don was having big problems, the kind Dad and Mom couldn't accept, they still accepted him. Mom especially, could hug my brother and touch him in a loving way, and I believe that helped rehabilitate him.

Our skin is the largest organ of our body, yet the least exercised. Americans are nontouchers, but we can learn how to utilize a healing touch. I've learned to express my love by touching my husband and children all I can. When I kiss someone, I end with a pat, or I embrace and pat at the same time. I love to touch Kathy's cute little nose, or run my hands through Larry Don's hair.

In fact, sometimes I even touch strangers! So far I've never been slapped. Maybe I'll see a kid in a supermarket, playing one of those electronic games, and I absentmindedly give him or her a pat or a hug. Now that I'm used to doing it with my own kids, somehow I want to pass it on!

Joni Eareckson is a very special lady who's used to wheelchair living. Once she came to town, and Mom and I went to hear her. I read her book *Joni*—the first book I read on my own following my accident. I really love her a lot.

Anyhow, I stood by Joni's wheelchair and hugged her, stroked her arms, that sort of thing. She smiled at me and said, "You know, in my heart I know that feels good!"

That touched my heart. First of all, Kathy felt willing to caress her friend not as a fragile, breakable egg, but as any other human being. And second, though Joni no longer has sensation in her arms, she certainly still feels in her heart. She liked that touching. That really ministered to me.

So many people are desperate to be touched, but we walk right on by. There are people in our own homes who need to be touched, hugged, kissed, stroked. . . . We should ask God to teach us to be willing to learn just how to touch.

Mothers and daughters could learn sometimes just to hold hands for a minute. Fixing the other's hair—zipping her dress—a little kiss good-bye—these cause good feelings in both people. It gets to be a habit. It brings you both closer.

Then there's tone of voice. My mom has a beautiful voice, and so does Dad. You get the right feeling about yourself when you hear love in someone's voice.

Mom believes it's very important to learn how to communicate. She teaches Larry Don and me to verbalize at a feeling level. When something bothers me, in other words, tell her what I feel. I really enjoy having the freedom to do that, especially since so many kids don't have that freedom. Their parents force them to keep their feelings bottled up.

We're learning how to defuse that dynamite! Feelings, after all, are neither good nor bad—they're just there. If I manage to demonstrate one thing to our kids, it's that they can learn to handle their emotions. They don't have to cover them over, deny them, or let their emotions rule their lives. Proverbs 16:32 says, "He that is slow to anger is better than the mighty; and he that ruleth his spirit than he that taketh a city."

Every one of us has to learn how to express our emotions and handle our feelings with care.

When people ask if Mom and I ever fuss and I say rarely, they say it sounds like an impossible relationship. But we rarely find ourselves in arguments or disagreements, and I think it's because we work on the feelings between us. Nothing gets blown out of proportion. Good feelings get expressed. We enjoy expressing them, because they make us feel good about ourselves, too.

When a child does or says something that makes a parent feel terribly threatened, I've learned there's a definite process the parent can utilize. When my kid hits on a real sore spot, when I get really defensive, there's a good chance it's rapped the little child inside me right across the knuckles! I need to look inside and see if there's a long-ago hurt that needs some attention.

What then? We can thank God for our new awareness. Until we become aware of our need in that area, we deny our hurt, disguise our hurt, or shove it under the rug. We don't talk about it. Even worse, we don't acknowledge it within ourselves.

The next step is to forgive. Forgive the person who inflicted that hurt, and forgive myself for my lifelong reactions toward that person and the hurt itself. Truly, no healing can take place until the forgiveness is given.

Thank God, as our children live their lives before us, our own childhood needs are mirrored in them. We can now approach and deal with these needs as our kids are used of God to reveal what needs to be revealed.

Another thing, Mom doesn't believe in talking and nagging us to death. Take the matter of chores. She used to give us verbal instructions, which caused arguments. Then Mom began making two separate lists—one for Larry Don, one for me. She posted them in the kitchen, and we checked off our jobs as we got them done.

Maybe we'd want to cut out somewhere with some kids. Mom would say, "Look at your list. How are you doing on your chores today?"

If they were done, fine. Go ahead and go. If not, we didn't need to argue with her. Just get down and do them. That was a good technique, since it eliminated a lot of so-called normal fussing. It put the responsibility on us, not on Mom.

That plan also works with husbands! Men are such bottom-line individuals. They want us to state a request, ask a question, get to the meat of what we want. Women, on the other hand, will spend thirty minutes building a case for them-

selves and set the stage for those men to get really exasperated.

I started writing a little agenda when I had things on my mind. I'd ask Larry for ten minutes of his time, at his convenience, and when he saw I had a little list of things to ask him, he respected me for that. He treated me with real consideration, because I was respecting his time. That one simple thing saved a lot of hurt feelings at our house.

I like feeling reinforced in a positive way. When Mom and I ride around town doing errands at the bank, the grocery store, wherever, we see people tearing each other down.

It's sad. I hate to hear a mother call her own child *stupid,* for example. That only reflects on *her!* But think how few times in public you see a mother reinforce her kids in a loving way, telling them how neat they are, and so forth.

When you continually assure someone he is okay, that you appreciate him, that you love and really need him, you're meeting some really basic needs in him. Conversely, there's the mother who's yelling, "Get over here. I told you not to go away. That's stupid . . . you're going to get hit with a car. . . ." Give a kid enough put-downs like that, and he'll live up to his mother's expectations.

We're told in the Bible to speak the truth in love. (Ephesians 4:15). Mom also quotes Proverbs 31:26 a lot: "She openeth her mouth with wisdom; and in her tongue is the law of kindness." She and I talk quite a bit about how much tearing down we can do with our tongues, or how we can use those same tongues for positive reinforcement!

Another thing Mom learned to do is, when you have a tough subject to discuss, meet somewhere outside of home to do it. She learned that almost all arguments take place in the kitchen or bedroom! So Mom has a strategy. She makes a date with Dad, or Larry Don or me—or maybe all three!—when she needs to talk about something that might hit you at your pressure points.

For example, if you need to talk about your schoolwork, Mom isn't going to yell at you about your grades when you're seated in some nice restaurant; and you're not going to go stomping off mad, either. Just changing environment takes the anger or impoliteness out of the situation.

Come to think of it, we do eat out a lot! (Just kidding, Mom.)

I believe most marriages would improve dramatically if we wives would decide not to let arguments happen in the bedroom. That's a terrible place to have arguments!

There's a lot to this subject of feelings. I know plenty of girls who think their mothers are jealous of them and their fathers. The mothers think the fathers prefer the daughters. That would be a tough problem, I believe.

Some mothers seem jealous of their daughters' beauty, affection expressed between father and daughter, or, very often, their daughter's ability to manipulate the father's emotions.

That comes from low self-esteem. When a woman knows she is right with God, herself, and her husband, there's no need for conflict between mother and daughter. That's a tool of Satan.

I've had so many mothers say to me, "We're just going through some normal mother-daughter conflicts." They talk as though the moment the child hits her teens, God has designed her to go into rebellion; that it's part of His plan. God did not design a family for disharmony. So much of what some psychologists and other so-called experts teach us simply can't be found in the Word of God, and we seem so willing to take their word as gospel—and not His!

Feelings. Mom and I had a good time making up a list of stuff to cover in this chapter. We've had a good time talking these things over in the past, experimenting with certain ideas, trying new ways to handle problems.

Mom's real close friend, Dick Dennis, who went to be with the Lord shortly after my accident, taught Mom something neat about how to handle feelings. Dick said, "Simply envision a circle of love around people when they're being difficult. Just step back and visualize them inside a warm circle, surrounded by God's love." Mom prays a circle of love around Larry Don and me, and has taught me to do the same thing. It feels great!

Learning to handle feelings can be really enjoyable. It feels wonderful to overcome those roadblocks with your parents or your children. Taking one thing at a time, here are some things to do.

ROADBLOCK OVERCOMERS

1. *Learn to reach out to others*—especially if they're "different." Old people, helpless people, little kids, all appreciate a helping hand, and are ready to love you back!

2. *Learn to be a "toucher."* It might seem strange at first, but it really builds a great bridge of communication. Even if you're angry with your mom, or if a woman is angry with her husband or her child, a gentle touch or a hug can make the whole thing much easier for everybody.

3. *Start touching in small, simple ways.* Fix your mother's hair for her. Take your daughter's hand when you come downstairs, or cross the street. Straighten your dad's tie. People like attention.

4. *Learn how to describe your feelings in words.* Parents need to let their kids do that. Children also need to learn how to listen to their parents and not tune them out. Adults also have feelings!

5. *We need to learn how to forgive.* When someone hurts your feelings, it's important to tell him—and then to say you forgive him. Forgiveness heals those hurts.

6. Instead of talking and starting a fuss, *write down family instructions in a memo or a list.* That avoids a lot of misunderstanding and hassling.

7. *Practice reinforcing others with sincere comments.* I like to drop a little card or love note sometimes, too. We all need encouragement. We also need to help others feel good about themselves.

8. *Try to find someplace other than home to discuss subjects that might start people arguing.* Talking about school, or job, or behavior—subjects that get people feeling threatened—can be discussed outside your

home. That way, nobody gets so angry it turns into a bad scene.

9. *Where there's jealousy, we need to work on our own low self-esteem.* Make a list of ten assets you find in yourself. Parents and children don't need to let something like jealousy drive them apart. Let God heal all that. Drive the old green-eyed monster away!

10. *Visualize people in a circle of love.* If someone attacks you verbally, or makes you feel insecure some other way, just step back and imagine Jesus drawing a ring around that person. When you imagine that love, it makes you want to come closer yourself!

We're learning to choose our feelings. Satan wants to attack us with negatives, but God helps us build up the positives.

Me? I'm feeling great. Fantastic! Definitely terrific . . . tremendous. It's a beautiful, glorious day!

14
Mom's Miracle

Some eight months ago, I realized my mother would be part of this book. That thought struck me with some force, since at first she didn't seem to "fit in," really. After all, my first impetus had been to share the wonderful, deep relationship God had established between Kathy and me. By contrast, my relationship to Mom had been far less "wonderful."

For some months I sifted memories concerning Mom and me—some funny—others so threatening or painful that I had to turn my mental eyes aside, and still others that were vivid, tender, and sentimental. I saw a fascinating woman, her life a mixture of sunlight and shadows. Did anyone really know Doris Barlow? Probably not, I decided. I felt quite sure she didn't really know herself.

Then circumstances tumbled a challenging opportunity into my lap, via a phone call from Mom's neighbor, then another from her nurse. "What shall we do with her?" they wanted to know. "I can't keep a night nurse. She's too sick to stay alone. What does your family prefer to do about this?"

Obviously the time had come for us to enter Mom into a nursing-home facility. Everyone hesitated to tackle the assignment, since all of us knew she'd refuse the move. Sick or not sick, Doris Barlow fully intended to run her own life, thank you!

Since I'd been dealing with Mom's doctors, nurses, and medications, I was the logical one to help her make the transition to her new life-style. I flew to California, determined to love her into the change and asking Jesus to help us help her. What a challenge! I knew my mom could fight for what she wanted—and she *wanted* her freedom and independence. That magnificent, lionhearted little lady would prove to be quite a handful, I predicted.

We didn't know the half of it. I knew it would take a lot of effort to persuade Mom of what we must do, but I had no idea of the physical stamina it would require of me. (I had just six days in which to do it all.) Meanwhile, I was constantly encouraging Mom that we *had* to make this move. It was not negotiable. It was the only move the doctor recommended.

It was painful. It was liberating. And during those days in which we worked and visited, I found myself able to perceive my mom with a brand-new set of eyes. That new vision sometimes felt exhilarating, often disturbing—but we both knew we were moving forward in our relationship.

Nevertheless, despite her severe breathing problems, pain, and inability to rest, Mother could argue incessantly against the necessity for the move. One day I confronted her, reluctantly, as she sat bolt upright in the upholstered chair she occupied. She looked tiny and outraged, as she once again railed at me in the old accustomed way, her blue eyes blazing with anger, her body rigid. Mom never changed.

However, Barbara *had* changed. Because of Kathy, I had learned to be transparent, to speak the truth in love. Mom might not understand, but that's the way it had to be.

"You can't talk to me that way!" she gasped. "You don't love me. You never loved me."

The Lord helped me walk past that old ploy without once looking back. "I do love you," I told her gently. "I always will love you. Mother, the most important thing in the world is, *God loves you.* He wants to help you with the problems within yourself."

She looked trapped and so pitifully vulnerable. It would have been so easy just to let it all go—to rationalize that it really didn't matter now—she was too old, too sick to change—but Jesus helped me hang in there. The same truths that pulled Kathy through must serve my sick, wandering, clever-minded mother. Sick and hurting as she was, I noticed with one corner of my mind, she still tried to manipulate her daughter!

For several days, Jesus and I ministered to Mom. We talked, my mother and I, at greater depth and intensity than at any other time in my life. These sickbed visits had been regular affairs—yet this one was different. This was a new Barbara, with a new attitude, and certainly a new belief that God wanted my mother delivered from her world of unreality and neurotic control over her children.

As I questioned her, Mother talked. She shared her fear and despair over disappointment in marriage, in life with an alcoholic. She loved my father so much, she said, and he had failed her—had failed us all. As she described her feelings, I felt my own overtones of grief. Had I not shared a little of these same feelings—disappointment, broken dreams, whatever—toward my own husband? And as my mother described how she had yearned for divorce, could I not relate to that? Had I not felt perfectly justified in my decision to walk out on my marriage?

In Mother's case, however, divorce certainly seemed justified. Why had she never gone forward with it? I knew she loved Dad, and he loved her, but what about us kids? What possible good could come from rearing four children in such ongoing emotional turmoil? We knew she loved us. We knew Dad loved us, too. Why, for everyone's sake, had Mother not faced facts, I asked. With Dad's drinking and all the other personality factors, we'd never had a viable family unit. Her answer stunned me.

"I was married twice before. I could not stand to see a third marriage end. It was bad—but I could never divorce him."

There followed a confession concerning a youthful Doris, unappreciated at home, marrying too young in order to escape her unhappiness, only to divorce in order to escape abusive treatment. There followed a second marriage only too much like the first—a heart-tearing account of a confused, troubled, young victim of circumstances.

No wonder she stuck by my father! Except for his drinking, he never abused her. Then, too, he loved her—clearly he must have loved her, to accept a woman with two failures behind her—a divorced woman, moreover, in an era when divorce seemed scandalous. So many things about my parents suddenly began to make sense. Pieces of the puzzle fell into place. And as she talked, as she aired long-gone memories, voiced her explanations, the Spirit of God led me to help her understand, somehow, that she must forgive herself. She must let go of the past, with all its enormous failures.

"Mom, God loves you," I told her. "These mistakes—we all make them—are gone. The blood of Jesus Christ covers every sin you and I, and all mankind, will ever commit. God has forgiven you, Mom. Now you must forgive yourself."

Bit by bit I began to share with my mother the principles God had given me, as I sought Him for my own identity. As I explained these things to Mom, I saw eagerness and hope begin to build in her bright little face.

"Where do I begin?" she asked me.

"The first place to start is in deciding you want to do it," I told her. "God will help you control your need for drugs. He can heal your body. He definitely will help you adapt to a new life in a new place, help you bless all the others who live there, and He'll give you new love, peace, and joy.

"We'll be praying for you, Mom. We're pulling for you. We want you to win!"

She nodded. Tears gathered in her brilliant blue eyes, eyes that still looked amazingly alert and young. *My mother is beautiful,* I thought. Then, startled, I realized something else. *I look just like her!* I looked full into her face for a long, tender moment, loving her and loving what I saw.

That began the *really* real relationship between Doris Barlow and Barbara Joanne Barlow Miller. A new respect developed between us. I offered Mom tough love, encouraging her, as earlier I had encouraged my own daughter. *Mom, with God's help, you're gonna win!*

It seemed very easy now for me to relate to this feisty little lady. God had helped me understand some basics about myself. Now they carried over to my mother. It was simple enough to recognize her basic lack of self-worth—and that of her mother before her.

Feelings of worthlessness like those my young mother

carried could topple any marriage, I reflected. What's more, her wild mood swings, deep depressions, and sudden tirades could easily drive a man to drink. Trapped in their own unresolved conflicts, each parent had aided the other in a downward spiral—a spiral each was helpless to halt.

Dear Lord, is it possible for someone my mother's age to change? Can she ever find happiness in this life?

Something in me believed Mom's spirit would triumph. I felt convinced she was approaching a new freedom, total peace, a release from her own personality traps. As we visited by phone or my infrequent letters, I encouraged her to go for it.

The new nursing home was good for her. Her life had order now, new friends, compassionate professionals, comfort. I praised mother's business astuteness. She had taken the money Dad left her, invested it wisely, and could live comfortably on the income she'd thus provided. I felt proud of my mother, proud of her energy and resourcefulness.

Her death did not shock me. She slipped away in her sleep during a bout with the flu, just weeks following the conversations in which for the first time I began to know her.

Praise God! He gave me my "real" mother, the woman I could so readily understand—the tiny, high-spirited lady with flashing blue eyes—the young girl who'd been hurt deeply, yet rallied to nurture four youngsters as best she could.

God gave me the "real" Doris, and He gave me my Self in so doing. I saw the woman from whom I came, and I loved her. And in loving her, I loved myself.

A miracle for Mom? I'd dared to believe God for it, and Kathy had too. *Thank You, Lord. Thank You, for giving my mother a piece of Kathy's miracle. Thanks for giving her new life!*

15

We're Gonna Win

Just about the time I felt ready to give up on our marriage, God gave me a message through a tree. I saw it standing in a field, totally bare. How could anything look so dead, so barren?

Suddenly I recognized that tree as one of the most beautiful in our area—a spreading, gloriously full tree when it buds and leafs out every spring. *When spring comes, that tree will be beautiful,* I thought. *I don't condemn that tree during its winters. . . .*

My mind leaped across a huge chasm to grasp an overwhelming thought. *Larry is in the winter of his years. He looks barren, stripped down, dead, but that's not true. God is working in his life. If God can work in a tree and cause such beauty to burst forth each spring, how much more can I believe He is working in Larry.*

That's really what happened. There are times in life when we can't feel or see life within us, but the fact is, it's there. Surely we could see no life in our damaged Kathy, we had to take it by faith. Through her I certainly understood that it's not what you see, or what you feel, it's what you know.

At the time of Kathy's accident, Larry seemed so in bondage, so boxed in, I couldn't reach him, no matter how hard I tried. Because he was approaching forty and not head of his company, unhappy in his work, heartbroken about

Kathy, estranged from his wife, and a son going ever deeper into drugs, he could not have been happy about himself.

When I offered Larry sincere compliments, he seemed incapable of receiving them. He was not receptive to my thoughts, or to me.

Women married to men in that position need to love them unconditionally. I did not do that. One day, as I showered, I was thinking of our family's story, which I told publicly so often after Kathy's miracle occurred. Each time I spoke, I stressed the importance of loving unconditionally, and that day the thought popped into my head that I had not loved my husband that way.

I really do love Larry, I thought, surprised. Then another thought popped up. *Do you? Do you really give him unconditional love, or do you tell him you'll love him* when *or if he does something?*

I began to realize I had not offered Larry Miller anything like unconditional love! Instead, I wanted some emotional return on my love investment, not understanding that Larry simply didn't have it to give at that time. Since I felt my needs weren't being met, even as I tried hard to meet the many needs of my family, I continually put conditions on my love for Larry.

Today, knowing what I now know, I'd say, don't put a string on that love. *I accept you, Larry, just as you are.* Through prayer, great things can happen. By working on my own area of life—*me*—by learning who I am and what my identity and self-esteem require, working on communication among us, somehow things changed.

I remember one big change, in particular. Some three weeks into Kathy's coma, Larry looked like a time bomb waiting to explode. He had so many pent-up feelings, with no way to let his misery out. That night I shared with him that I had relinquished Kathy into God's care, and asked him if he wanted to do the same.

"I don't know how," he choked, and began to cry like a baby. As I led Larry in his prayer of relinquishment, I thought I'd never in all my life seen anyone cry so hard.

The "Neuro" ward where Kathy lay held so much trauma. After the night I prayed with Larry, I often saw him willing to offer emotional help to others. One night a lady died, and we saw her husband simply standing in the hall, looking so lost and upset. You could see he wanted to cry, but didn't know how. Larry went to him and embraced him tenderly, and the gentleman began to weep. My strong, stoical husband, who always had been so undemonstrative, showing such compassion—I wanted to weep, myself.

All this was new to Larry. He never had known how to show his emotions. What's more, after years of watching Larry and Larry Don exhibit anger and hostility to one another, it always thrills me to see them embrace. They hug one another so freely and unself-consciously. To God be the glory!

That's a far cry from the Larry I first knew, a man unwilling to hug me in public, lest someone consider him unmasculine. Now he's the world's best hugger. He hugs men *and* women. In fact, the gals absolutely stand in line for Larry's hugs, because he's so warm and strong, and when he hugs you, you *know* you've been hugged!

Thank God I waited for Larry's "Spring" to break through. It has been glorious! To the woman who identifies with my old feelings of emotional need: deprivation—lack of loving support, as I saw it—I'd say, yes, God can make the same thing happen in your home, too. It's worth the wait!

As God trained me to a patient, new work with Kathy, I clearly saw that self-esteem and self-belief can't be built in a day. As she began her life again at the very beginning, I saw we all must begin our new life in Christ the same way—step-by-step. Obviously, I offered her every kind of positive reinforcement, and I saw her thrive.

That daily practice helped me understand that a man needs constant reinforcement. You can tell him he's the apple of your eye—you desire him—his body is attractive—yet unless you're reinforcing him in all the basic ways that really matter, he can't receive your words.

At first, Larry shrugged away my kind words—my sincerest compliments. But God was working a work not just in Kathy, who had been wounded almost unto death, but in every other one of us—each one equally wounded in his spirit, and fighting equally hard for life. Because Kathy's wounds were visible, we continually encouraged her with the words, "You're gonna win, with God's help."

Gradually, those words settled into my spirit and lodged there. Deep in my heart I knew, "With the Lord's help, we're all gonna win!"

The slogan began to spread. Dick Dennis, the closest male friend I ever loved, particularly appreciated it. As I mentioned before, Dick himself was fighting against cancer. In fact, he and his wife, June, my closest friend, were scheduled to leave town just before Kathy's accident, then canceled because Dick was battling pain. Despite his own condition, he came to us at the hospital, and ministered to Larry and me. What devotion!

Following the race that catapulted Kathy into national (and even international) attention, Dick noticed a tee shirt advertised in a sports magazine and commissioned June to find one for Kathy. June scoured the shops, and found the shirt Dick wanted in a local tennis shop—just an ordinary white tee shirt, emblazoned with the words I'M GONNA WIN.

Kathy loved it. She wore the shirt everywhere. It so reinforced everything we'd been saying, that with God's help we were going to win, that I had more shirts printed. I felt others needed that message as much as we did. I also had the slogan printed on buttons, and when we visit a school we pass these out.

We're called to spread the Gospel, and I believe "I'm Gonna Win" presents the Good News in capsule form. It's the most *positive* statement. Everybody wants to be a winner. Kathy has received tee-shirt requests from everywhere. Men wear them. Women wear them. Little kids all ages, shapes, and sizes wear them—and it thrills us.

In Christ, every person becomes a winner. In the world, however, people seem to think it's always *either/or*—you win, or you lose. When Kathy speaks to groups, she always says you don't have to come in first to be a winner. Rather, God wants you to do your best with what you've got, and complete the race.

That's *winning!*

We stayed in the race, Larry and I, though I doubt that either of us could foresee any spectacular finish. Still, there were signs. For example, I recall the surprising honor of being nominated and then chosen as Arizona's "Mother of the Year" in 1979.

You can imagine my gratitude, both to God and to others.
But in all that, the award of all awards came through a simple book my husband and children presented to me. Larry
had gone to the trouble to collect all the letters and docu-
ments pertaining to my nomination, the pictures and news
articles, which he had copied and bound in book form. If I
were touched by that thoughtfulness, I felt overwhelmed by
my husband's inscription:

> *Barbara:* A tremendous amount of love, joy, and pride
> has gone into preparing this. For me to be able to
> express what you've meant to me all these years, to
> read how much you've influenced so many other lives
> has been one tremendous experience for me.
>
> I hope you'll enjoy and cherish this extra copy of your
> nomination—so much love went into preparing it from
> so many people; and the best part is that all these let-
> ters of nomination really echo the feelings and
> thoughts of hundreds of other people. You are truly an
> uncommon woman.
>
> Love, LARRY

As I copy Larry's words, I remind myself for the millionth
time—*he was worth the wait.*

We continued to learn, he and I. We learned to touch,
learned to feel, learned to communicate. And as I watched
Larry open up and change, I began to discover a man I'd
never known. For example, I knew he had deep and tender
feelings—feelings so deep he had no idea how to let them
show. Still, I never dreamed he had such worlds of unex-
pressed love—such unimagined yearnings—toward *me.*

Sometimes Larry astounds me. Released, free in Jesus Christ to be exactly who he is, he exhibits almost boundless enthusiasm and the kind of imagination that would excite any woman. Consider the matter of my fortieth birthday, for example. It might not surprise any woman reading this to learn that Larry staged a surprise party to mark my attaining the "Big Forty." It surprised me, though, to the point of rendering me absolutely speechless when literally dozens of our friends burst in, laughing and singing "Happy Birthday."

You see, Larry doesn't do that sort of thing—but he did. What's more, it was all his idea. My friend who hosted the party offered to handle all details, but Larry declined. He handled the invitations, ordered the food, made all arrangements.

It worked like a charm. Not only was I surprised, I was *flabbergasted.* Larry's *pièce de résistance,* however, was a game he had devised. Several guests received a short verse which offered clues leading to the next guest. My own verse led to Larry, of course, and also instructed me to follow a red ribbon which wound from room to room throughout the house—through the kitchen and into the carport.

I like games. We all laughed and cut up, as I followed the ribbon, enjoying our closeness, our silliness, still thrilled at Larry's producing such a surprise—and *then I saw it.* Brand-new, pristine, red-ribbon wrapped. There sat the smartest little sea-green sports convertible you ever saw. Totally unexpected, something I'd never dreamed of owning, a gift unimaginably lavish—what in the world can I say to describe my overwhelming feelings at that moment?

Thank You, Lord, for an experience that unforgettable.
Sure, I love the car—you'd better believe it. What woman
wouldn't enjoy such an automobile? But such enjoyment
dwindles into total insignificance beside the intangibles that
car represents. Every time I drive it, I remember that
night—the shock of joy I felt—and most of all, Larry's face,
lit with love for me.

I'm learning to know the man, and it's exciting. It isn't all
happening overnight, but what love affair does? The day I
turned forty, I realized again—I hardly know Larry at all.
There are depths to him, possibilities in him, I can't begin to
dream of. Only as I release him, stop trying to be his mother,
allow him to find himself, can I know and truly love the man
God chose for me.

Is this hope unrealistic? Can we, in fact, change as much
as we actually need to change? My mind flashes back to a
scene in a London television station, when our British interviewer asked Kathy if her plan to attempt a certain achieve-
ment might not turn out to be "unrealistic."

As we all pondered a reply, Larry Don fired back a statement: "Let's look at it this way. It seems 'unrealistic' that
Kathy can sit or stand, walk or talk, or do any of these other
things they said she'd never do. We don't deal with the word
unrealistic. We simply ask Kathy for what we need from her."

We had to learn, Kathy and I, the visual technique of be-
lieving something before you have it. I called it positive
visualization. No matter where Kathy was in the here and
now, I asked God to quicken my mind as to where she could
be. I painted verbal pictures for her. We visualized where
she was going.

I believe that's a tremendous tool for building any relationship. You can visualize where it's going and talk it into existence. Later we were able to do the same thing with Larry Don. At his very lowest, I could tell him, with conviction, "I know God's hand is on your shoulder. You're going to be free of these drugs and become the marvelous man He intends you to be."

I said that over and over and over.

With Larry, I had to start by deciding that I wanted to be in a position to try to love him. Convinced our love was dead, our marriage hopeless, my own starting place had to be within myself. As Larry would say, I needed to be willing to be willing!

I won't pretend it's easy for me or anyone else to practice "positive visualization" in a situation like ours. It takes determination. I began to "see" Larry as a fine leader, a strong head of our house, and I told him so. I praised him for the way he handled certain challenges, expressed gratitude for the good provision he'd always made for our household, and encouraged him by saying I could see him becoming a Diamond . . . a Double Diamond . . . a Triple Diamond . . . a Crown . . . would you believe, a Crown Ambassador in our own Amway business? (These are titles of outstanding achievements in our Amway business organization.)

Now those would have been just so many words, had I not truly understood that with God, all things are possible. As Jesus said, "If thou canst believe, all things are possible to him that believeth" (Mark 9:23).

Today I see the outcome of that positive visualization, and it's so exciting. After Larry Don, Kathy, and I began to pray for God to bless Larry with added love, and the gift of

His Holy Spirit, in due season Larry made Jesus the Lord of his life. Typically, it was a quiet and private transaction on Larry's part. But also typically, God immediately began to produce a radiance, a freedom, and a winsomeness in this man that makes his personality virtually irresistible.

Larry has picked up on those reinforcing techniques, by the way, and by the force of his loving leadership helps our family to strengthen, day by day. We are so happy. When I phoned home yesterday to ask a question, he remarked, "I'm so proud of you. I knew you could do it," referring to some decision I'd made.

His encouragement feels so good. Those are the exact kind of strokes I've needed so long—and so desperately. In my younger years, longing to be told how important and precious I was, when I didn't yet know who I really was—how much I needed the kind of man my Larry has become. I praise God for him.

In my mind, I collect snapshots. Recently I saw a scene: a family portrait, except for me—and my mental camera went *click!* They are walking across a parking lot, coming away from a basketball game. It has just rained, the pavement is wet, and the outdoor lights sparkle and reflect against all that wetness.

There they come, my three loves—Larry, Larry Don, and Kathy walking between them. They're holding hands, laughing and kidding, their faces lit like candles. When they come to puddles, Larry Don scoops Kath into his arms and jumps across. I hear her squealing. . . .

Those "snapshots" are precious. The laughing faces—the birthday party, with all my friends—that wildly extravagant gift—how can you top such things?

Still, God did it. In fact, He does it, again and again. He is the author of every good and perfect gift! Last Mother's Day, returning from California dead-tired, little did I dream what all our God had laid up for me—and for all of us.

I'd ministered to Mom, and felt so grateful to be home again. *It would be nice to rest, to simply be quiet,* I thought. That would be the finest gift I could possibly receive.

My family did not agree. We had dinner reservations in Sedona, they said, at my very favorite restaurant. I groaned inside, fatigued at the thought of a two-hour drive to beautiful, mountainous Sedona. Four hours of driving that afternoon, just for dinner!

"Could I have a rain check?"

One look at their faces, and I knew that question was a bummer. We drove to Sedona, but my heart certainly was not in it. Once there, however, I began to enter in. My family is undeniably charming, and they were out to give me a really good time on Mother's Day. There were flowers for me, a delightful dinner, good fellowship, and sharing. Obviously they were glad to see Mom come home. I had to respond to that!

Now Sedona, Arizona, happens to be one of the single most beautiful areas in the United States, in my opinion. The openness, the vast skies, the towering rock formations—all that desert beauty makes my soul almost gasp for breath sometimes. I never want to leave such majesty and peace. That day, however, tired as I was, I just wanted to go home. I couldn't understand why they couldn't understand that—why they insisted on driving around, looking at just one house.

In Sedona, we always looked at houses, drove up winding

trails to inspect still another mountain, yet another view. We never seemed to tire of it. This time, despite my weariness, my heart lifted once again. The house sat high, overlooking rough desert terrain, the road leading to "town," and ring after ring of mountains that seemed to stretch to the rim of the world.

The house was open, and we walked through, exclaiming at its features. I liked the spacious rooms, so airy and peaceful—the beautiful fireplace—the indescribable view from the deck that wrapped itself nearly around the entire house. . . .

"Let's rest on the porch a while," Larry suggested. Outside, he handed me a Mother's Day card.

"Shall I open this now?" I asked.

"Yes, do." So I entered into their ritual once more, reading a sweet, printed message, then the one scribbled in Larry's bold hand:

BARBARA, WE HOPE YOU LIKE THIS HOUSE, BECAUSE IT IS
OURS. WE LOVE YOU. . . .

I felt absolutely faint. Weeping with joy, I asked a million questions . . . how? . . . when? . . . and they laughed at me as they explained. They'd discovered the house (Larry and Kathy), while I was away. We'd been seeking a mountain retreat for some time. In fact, we'd almost closed one deal, and "our" house got away.

Then Larry and Kathy spotted this one. "Let's take it now," they decided, "before someone else does. We'll surprise Mom. She'll love it!" They were right, and they were right!

We dubbed our special house *La Place de la Paix*—The

Place of Peace," loosely translated from the French. It's impossible to describe what a gift it has been, since it so specifically meets all the desires of my heart. You see, for years I'd collected articles and ideas for just such a house, saved these in a folder, which nobody but God and me knew anything about. *La Place* contains so many of my dream-house ideas—things neither Larry or Kathy could possibly have known: It makes me cry.

Moreover, how could my husband know me that well? How could he understand so perfectly the deepest desires within the hidden heart of Barbara Miller? Apart from God, he could not. That much I know.

The "old" Larry Miller could never have conceived the freedom to make such a bold purchase—to be so sure I'd be so totally enraptured—and to be so *right*.

Lord, this is the lavish love I always wanted—the tenderness I needed so long—everything I could ever imagine, from the only man I ever loved. . . .

Of course, it is a mystery. God's ways are far above our ways, and all love is of God.

Don't think, however, that Barbara Miller learned her lessons so well that all stays rosy. Don't for one moment believe that the "old" Barbara with the old fears, doubts, and controlling spirit, never hangs around anymore. That's simply not true. We all have to maintain a constant vigil, or the old negatives tend to crowd back in. Praise the Lord, anyhow!

As someone has said, "Without battles, there are no victories." One victory happened just weeks ago, after I telephoned Larry at work and tried to make a date with him for lunch. He had a conflict, and I felt disappointed.

Within moments, however, he rang me back. He'd love to have lunch with me after all. I felt glad, and I could hear a similar gladness in his voice.

"What's with you, Mr. Miller? You sound excited!"

"Well, Barb, I didn't mean to tell you until we met, but. . . ." And with increasing excitement, Larry told me he had decided to resign his vice-president's position. His voice rang with freedom and vitality, and I simply laughed aloud. How amazing! Few men could know themselves so well they'd decided to walk away from a job that well paying, that rewarding and prestigious. *Hallelujah! Larry was free!*

When my husband entered our Amway business full-time, Larry Don decided to come in also and complete our family's involvement with a thriving system I'd begun so long ago, during my earliest search for identity. What an amazing outcome for us all! I felt elated.

Meanwhile, back to real life. Together the four Millers began to create something brand-new from what had started, a dozen years earlier, as "Mom's business." I thought Larry, with his captivating personality, vibrant voice and real talent for motivating and inspiring others, had to be the most marvelous asset you could ever ask for. As for Larry Don and Kathy—well, I'm prejudiced. The truth is, I believe we're all fantastic winners. Thank You, Lord! Amway has a way of making you feel good about each other—and yourself.

Larry Don's involvement remained part-time, of course, since he had a satisfying regular job. From Day One he made excellent progress in the company, set and met his goals by dint of real vision and discipline. I felt so excited for him at first, but then noticed he was slacking off.

Not only was Larry Don no longer setting any records, by now he was becoming downright undependable. At home, in his job, in our business, our son had begun to slip—and I had begun to question him. At last, thoroughly steamed up by his failure to show up at a meeting he said he'd attend, I confronted him.

"Larry Don, you disappointed everybody last night," I began. "You're terrific in your new business. You got off to such a great start and displayed such a warm personality that you can't help but win. You've got what it takes, very obviously.

"Then suddenly you become haphazard. We have an important meeting and you don't show. You let us down, and you really don't even have a valid excuse or reason.

"Son, I love you. I admire you and I'm proud of you—but you're acting like a jerk!"

It had taken me ten days to arrive at this confrontation. *From the day of Mom's funeral until now,* I thought, *I've been trying to get Larry Don and me into some kind of framework.* At *La Place,* quiet before God, the Lord touched me and said my problem was my need to control.

Now we stood in the kitchen. Larry Don looked down at me, wondering if this were a full-scale attack, figuring how to answer. I stood, thoroughly provoked, trying to read that sensitive young face, trying just to *get along* with the young man.

I knew what I needed to do, and the words fairly flew from my mouth. "Larry Don, you're a young man, not a child. You don't need a mother to tell you how to live your life. From now on, I'll be glad to give you my opinions and leave the choices to you. Please forgive me for trying to control you. I don't have that right.

"Larry Don, I give you your freedom!"

He gazed at me narrowly. "You mean it?"

I wondered if he fully understood just what I was trying to say. "I really mean it, son. You are your own man from now on. You don't have to answer to me."

I felt something lift from my heart and take off on wings. I saw relief slide across Larry Don's face, too, as he began to laugh, kid, and caper around the kitchen. *Indeed, he does understand me,* I thought. *He looks like a brand-new man.*

Lord God, how hard it is sometimes to give You true control and not take things into my own hands!

Last night I dreamed the strangest dream—so vivid, so intense and in a way, so intriguing. Funny, I never remember dreams. In the morning, all details simply vanish. This one, however, cannot be put away. Despite all my intentions, it keeps returning to my mind and, for some reason, I feel it is unfinished—and I do not understand.

Why would I dream that Larry Don and I dug up my mother's body, opened her casket, and looked at her? Oh, it was not as gross as it sounds. In fact, it seemed a tranquil, peaceful dream. We dug up my mother's so recently buried body, and she looked beautiful. Larry Don and I looked at her and felt happy.

"I love you, Grandma," Larry Don said, in my dream. "I want you to know I relate to you. You were addicted as I was addicted, and I understand about your drugs.

"I love you, I really love you. I want you to know that."

My son *needed* to tell Mom those things, I saw with such aching love. He had poignant, unfinished business with her. The excitement mounted as, in the dream, Larry Don and I decided to call in Mom's neighbors and let them talk to her in the way I call "meadowing." They were explaining their feelings to my mother.

"Doris, I wanted to love you, but you didn't receive my love," one explained. "You always were so self-sufficient. When I tried to tell you and show you how I really felt, you flared up verbally and pushed me away."

"I always loved you, Doris, and I forgive you for the hostility you sometimes expressed to me," another neighbor said. Others told similar feelings, as Larry Don and I waited and watched. At last the parade ended, the scene was completed. We could replace my mother in the ground.

As I dreamed, I came into an overwhelming knowledge that none of the garbage was in the box with Mom. As I watched my son finish his work with my mother, saw her neighbors finish theirs, I felt an extraordinary freedom, peace, and joy that's impossible to describe.

That morning, as I dressed, wondering at myself, asking God to show me the meaning of that strange and vivid vision, I decided not to share it with anyone else. I had to hurry, anyhow. Larry Don's car was in the shop, and he and I had to drive there, then on to meet Larry for breakfast.

The moment Larry Don and I left home, wouldn't you know, I told him all about that dream! "You see, the 'junk' stops our relationships from being good," I explained with sudden insight. "None of the 'garbage' or the 'unfinished business' goes into the box with the one who dies. That person is free. But what about us, left here with junk to deal with? For us, we can go to Jesus for our meadowing. Jesus is the Mediator.

"Oh, Larry Don, see how important each person is to

God—how important to go to one another with those feelings—to knock down those barriers. . . ."

He understood. He simply nodded his head, flashing me a quick, sympathetic smile. It felt good, I realized, to be able to say you had no unfinished business to transact with anyone. If I were to die this afternoon—or if they went to be with the Lord right now—we didn't need to dig up that box.

No, I didn't need to dig up any boxes—except one. Larry's. I winced inside, recalling something that happened last night. I'd been digging through piles of family photos all afternoon, choosing pictures for this book. It had been tedious, and I'd need to work all evening.

"What's for dinner?" Larry asked from the doorway.

"I don't know. What are your plans this evening?"

"Don't have any," he said, smiling.

Most of our Amway business is conducted during the evenings. Here I was, fully occupied, and Larry had no plans. I began to have a bad-attitude attack, and chose to allow my martyr spirit to flare. "Look in the refrigerator, Larry. Find yourself something to eat. Can't you see I'm busy? Better still, why not go out to eat?"

As I heard the words leave my mouth, I knew they were wrong. It was too late, however. The set of Larry's shoulders, the slight slam of his car door, told me all I needed to know. I finished my work, depressed, and headed for bed alone.

Now we traveled toward our breakfast meeting. I could not escape the meeting, nor the conviction of what God would have me do. Larry sat comfortably, reading a newspaper, and at first didn't acknowledge our presence. The "old" Barbara would have said, "Hey, I'm here." Now I sat silently, waiting.

He laid the newspaper to one side almost immediately, flashed a big smile, and greeted us warmly. I knew what I must say, and that I must say it at the outset.

"Larry, I'm sorry about last night. I was wrong, and I need your forgiveness. I was trying to control you." He sat with his eyes riveted to mine, and I plunged on. "I've tried to control you in our Amway business. When I think you're not planning for our future, I'm afraid you're going to fail. I've tried to control you, so we wouldn't fail. I've tried to be your *mother.*"

I had Larry's full attention now, but I couldn't read his face. "What I want you to know is, you're free to succeed or fail. If we fail, I'll be by your side and go down the tubes with you. If you want to develop the business, super. If you want a nine-to-five job, that's okay, too.

"In other words, Larry, I give you your freedom!"

The reaction was immediate—and funny. "Larry Don, did you hear that? *Did you hear that?* She has given you your freedom, and now she's giving me mine. Hey, Sharon! [Our waitress.] Would you come over here and witness this? Barbara, would you get a notary public and put this in writing?"

We all laughed and got slapstick for a minute, but almost immediately Larry Don's eyes flew to his father's as he asked, "Dad, where do you stand?"

"You mean, how do I feel about receiving my freedom?"

"No." There was a slight pause. "Where are you about giving me *my* freedom?" our son asked.

"You know I want you to be free to do the things you want to do," Larry answered. Immediately Larry Don responded with some personal plans for his day off. As he outlined those ideas, I saw rebellion shoot up in my husband. He struggled with it a moment, then said, "I want to see you become all you can, because ..." and then he stopped. He heard himself putting a condition on that love.

He turned to me then, grinning. "I feel excited, honey. I like what you said."

"The truth is, Larry, I want some freedom myself," I told him. "There are some things I want to be and do."

He leaned toward me, genuinely interested. "What sort of things? I thought you did your own thing, Barbara."

"I believe I've been called of God to do some things," I responded slowly, amazed at the turn our conversation was taking. "Some writing, maybe, and more teaching and ministry. For five years I've wanted to be in an exercise program and said I couldn't because I was so busy taking care of everyone else's needs.

"The truth is, that's *not* the truth. I was copping out. I pure ol' didn't want to do it! Larry, I need some time for myself. I see Kathy so disciplined, so ready to do the things she really wants to do, and not only do I respect her for it, I get downright envious. When I tell her that, she comes right back at me. She says, 'Mother, it can be yours.' Larry, I want some freedom and I want you to be free, too."

He nodded his head, excited at the prospect, smiling and energetic and identifying with me. I believe we both will remember those moments.

We're gonna win. As I realized at breakfast, we only have freedom when we become willing to free others. With God's help, we can learn to love with no strings attached—*and we're gonna win!*

A tremendous excitement builds within me, as I recall the

ways a loving God has brought us to this point. I could burst
with gratitude. I could weep for joy.

Truly, He has a way for each person, each family, to
travel. Your story could be different from mine. Your life is
unique, your personality equally so. Just as He has saved
Larry, Larry Don, Kathy, and me, I know He cares as tenderly for every other individual and every family in the
world.

Jesus Christ is *real*. It is through Him that we can truly
know I'M GONNA WIN! Perhaps your heart is struggling with
deep hurts and problems, as you read these words. Perhaps
you identify with our family's desperate needs. Perhaps you
have suffered with damaged, wounded relationships.

Unless you know beyond a doubt, "I know Jesus. He died
for me," I'd say, let's invite Him this moment to become
part of your life. As you read this, I join with you:

> Dear God, I know I am a sinner. My life is empty,
> my relationships faulty, and I can't help myself. Also,
> I've done and said things for which I'm ashamed. But
> God, I know Jesus died for me, and because of that,
> You will forgive all my sins. Jesus, I ask You to come
> into my life. Take me as I am, and change me into the
> person You want me to be. Thank You for saving me. I
> ask You to become Lord of my life. *Amen.*

I thank God that you and I can become new persons in
Christ. We have gained a Friend who will stick closer than a
brother. He loves you. He loves me. So be it.